The American Indian:

The First Victim

EDITED BY JAY DAVID
The American Indian: The First Victim
Black Defiance
Growing Up Black

CO-EDITED BY JAY DAVID AND ELAINE CRANE
The Black Soldier
Living Black in White America

CO-EDITED BY JAY DAVID
To Be A Black Woman (*with Mel Watkins*)
Growing Up African (*with Helise Harrington*)

The American Indian

The First Victim

Edited by Jay David

William Morrow & Company, Inc., New York 1972

I thank my associate editor, Diane Berkowitz, for her work on this book.

Contents

Introduction

The aboriginal inhabitants of North America occupy a unique position in the history of this country. They were the first people on this continent, the land was theirs. These people, whom Columbus christened "Indians" in the mistaken belief that he had reached the East Indies, were not a monolithic group. Comprised of over three hundred language groupings, various societies were settled across the continent, each evolving a different culture, each suited to the land which sustained it.

White Europeans "discovered" the continent and a great and continuous conflict arose. The differences which fed this conflict, later to erupt in genocidal wars against the native peoples, were basic in their outlook upon life. The Indians had no form of writing in common usage, but the spoken word was highly valued. The Europeans, feeling that literacy was the mark of civilization, branded the natives as savages, innately inferior beings.

A second, and very important difference, was in the two groups' relation to land. To the Europeans land was a commodity to be owned and used. Land which was not included in some form of written title was free for the taking. The Indians' relation to the land was entirely different. Though various tribes occupied particular territories and recognized each others' boundaries, the right to land was a right to use it, not to own or buy and sell it. Further, the Indians had a great reverence for the land. In some Indian religions the land was thought of as the mother, nourishing and giving life to her children. The Indian would no more abuse or exploit the land than he would abuse or exploit a loved relative.

Thus the stage was set for the conflict which continues today. The "Manifest Destiny" of the white man decreed that he must push across the North American continent to the Pacific. The Indian cultures were ignored, the Indian considered a savage, unworthy of notice unless his lands were desired. In time, the United States Government made treaties with the Indians, buying some of their lands in return for tools and other implements of "civilization." In his quest for progress, for more land, the white man broke his treaties with the Indians, successively moving them out of their homes when their lands were wanted. In 1830, Congress passed the Indian Removal Act. The Cherokees, inhabitants of the mountain country where Georgia, Tennessee, and North Carolina meet, were required to move to the wilderness west of the Mississippi River. The Indians of the Southeast and Northwest were similarly "removed." When the native peoples resisted, the government countered with armed force. This was the prototypic situation that set off the series of wars between the Indians and whites which raged from 1840 to 1876.

The relationship between the Indian and the white in America has demanded the assimilation of the Indian, the denial of his culture. Rather than capitulating, the Indians have insisted on treatment as a separate people, having their own customs, cultures, and laws. The purpose of this book is to explore these facets of Indian life, to offer a forum in which the Indian himself will present a discussion of his own history, philosophy, and needs. For too long the white man has spoken for the Indian. It is time that non-Indians listen to the voices which they have long suppressed.

Jay David

New York City

I

Growing Up Indian

For the American Indian childhood was the most critical period of life. It was a time of play and adventure, but most importantly, it was the period of preparation for full participation in tribal life. In modern industrial societies childhood may be dismissed as a frivolous period preceding later serious training for a technical or professional career. This was not the case in native American societies. In these societies work was the total effort to survive. From birth, then, the Indian child learned the skills necessary for survival in the wilderness and also the responsibilities that his role as a member of a self-sustaining tribal society demanded. During childhood the Indian youth also learned the customs, legends, and traditions of his tribe. Morals and manners were not neglected. From infancy the child was expected to develop that greatness of character demanded by the tribe.

The early experiences of all Indian children were not the same, but varied with the geographical location and culture of the tribe. Similarly, the experiences of Indian childhood were greatly altered by the arrival of the white man and the disruptions of tribal life which ensued.

The following section includes accounts of Indian youth in various time periods and under varying historical conditions. The individuals whose stories are recounted also differed in the degree to which they were assimilated into white culture. The youthful hero depicted in the selection from N. Scott Momaday's *House Made of Dawn* enjoyed the free life of the Plains hunter. Okah Tubbee, stolen as a child from his Choctaw family and sold into slavery, was forced into assimilation. John Rollin's life was severely disrupted by the removal of his native Cherokee Nation from their natural home; he subsequently chose to live among the whites. Motivated by the pressures of white civilization, Black Elk left his reservation to tour the world with a Wild West show.

Though the experiences of these Indian youths varied, in their narratives can be seen the strength of character imbued in them by their Indian heritage.

1

FROM

House Made of Dawn

by N. Scott Momaday

For the Indians of the Plains hunting was not a sport but a necessity upon which the existence of the tribe depended. The hunter stalked and killed his prey with the skill of an artist and the reverence of a worshipper. In the following excerpt from his novel, House Made of Dawn, *N. Scott Momaday tells the story of a young man's first bear hunt. For this youth the hunt became a rite of initiation. Returning to his village with the bear, the boy returned home a man.*

A Kiowa Indian, N. Scott Momaday grew up on reservations in the Southwest. His first novel, House Made of Dawn, *won the 1969 Pulitzer Prize for literature. Currently Associate Professor of English and Comparative Literature at the University of California at Berkeley, Mr. Momaday is also the author of* The Way to Rainy Mountain, *published in 1969.*

. . . He was a young man, and he rode out on the buckskin colt to the north and west, leading the hunting horse, across the river and beyond the white cliffs and the plain, beyond the hills and the mesas, the canyons and the caves. And once, where the horses could not go because the face of the rock was almost vertical and unbroken and the ancient handholds were worn away to shadows in the centuries of wind and rain, he climbed among the walls and pinnacles of rock, adhering like a vine to the face of the rock, pressing with no force at all his whole mind and weight upon the sheer ascent, running the roots of his weight into invisible hollows and cracks, and he heard the whistle and moan of the wind among the crags, like ancient voices, and saw the horses far below in the sunlit gorge. And there were the caves. He came suddenly upon a narrow ledge and stood before the mouth of a cave. It was sealed with silver webs, and he brushed them away. He bent to enter and knelt down on the floor. It was dark and cool and close inside, and smelled of damp earth and dead and ancient fires, as if centuries ago the air had entered and stood still behind the web. The dead embers and ashes lay still in a mound upon the floor, and the floor was deep and packed with clay and glazed with the blood of animals. The chiseled dome was low and encrusted with smoke, and the one round wall was a perfect radius of rock and plaster. Here and there were earthen bowls, one very large, chipped and broken only at the mouth, deep and fired within. It was beautiful and thin-shelled and fragile-looking, but he struck the nails of his hand against it, and it rang like metal. There was a black metate by the door, the coarse, igneous grain of the shallow bowl forever bleached with meal, and in the ashes of the fire were several ears and cobs of corn, each no bigger than his thumb, charred and brittle, but whole and hard as wood. And there among the things of the dead he listened in the stillness all around and heard only the lowing of the wind . . . and then the plummet and rush of a great swooping bird—out of the corner of his eye he saw the awful shadow which hurtled across the light—and the clatter of wings on the cliff, and the small, thin cry of a rodent. And in the same instant the huge wings heaved with calm, gathering up the dead weight, and rose away.

All afternoon he rode on toward the summit of the blue mountain, and at last he was high among the falls and the steep timbered slopes. The sun fell behind the land above him and the dusk grew up among the trees, and still he went on in the dying light, climbing up to the top of the land.

And all afternoon he had seen the tracks of wild animals and heard the motion of the dead leaves and the breaking of branches on either side. Twice he had seen deer, motionless, watching, standing away in easy range, blended with light and shadow, fading away into the leaves and the land. He let them be, but remembered where they were and how they stood, reckoning well and instinctively their notion of fear and flight, their age and weight.

He had seen the tracks of wolves and mountain lions and the deep prints of a half-grown bear, and in the last light he drew up in a small clearing and made his camp. It was a good place, and he was lucky to have come upon it while he still could see. A dead tree had fallen upon a bed of rock; it was clear of the damp earth and the leaves, and the wood made an almost smokeless fire. The timber all around was thick, and it held the light and the sound of the fire within the clearing. He tethered the horses there in the open, as close to the fire as he could, and opened the blanket roll and ate. He slept sitting against the saddle, and kept the fire going and the rifle cocked across his waist.

He awoke startled to the stiffening of the horses. They stood quivering and taut with their heads high and turned around upon the dark and nearest wall of trees. He could see the whites of their eyes and the ears laid back upon the bristling manes and the almost imperceptible shiver and bunch of their haunches to the spine. And at the same time he saw the dark shape sauntering among the trees, and then the others, sitting all around, motionless, the short pointed ears and the soft shining eyes, almost kindly and discreet, the gaze of the gray heads bidding only welcome and wild good will. And he was young and it was the first time he had come among them and he brought the rifle up and made no sound. He swung the sights slowly around from one to another of the still, shadowy shapes, but they made no sign except to cock their heads a notch, sitting still and away in the darkness like a litter of pups, full of shyness and wonder and delight. He was hard on the track of the bear; it was somewhere close by in the night, and it knew of him, had been ahead of him for hours in the afternoon and evening, holding the same methodical pace, unhurried, certain of where it was and where he was and of every step of the way between, keeping always and barely out of sight, almost out of hearing. And it was there now, off in the blackness, standing still and invisible, waiting. And he did not want to break the stillness of the night, for it was holy and profound; it was rest and restoration, the hunter's offering of death and the sad watch of the hunted, waiting somewhere away in the cold darkness and breathing easily of its life, brooding around at last to forgiveness and consent; the silence was essential to them both, and it lay out like a bond between them, ancient and inviolable. He could neither take nor give any advantage of cowardice, where no cowardice was, and he laid the rifle down. He spoke low to the horses and soothed them. He drew fresh wood upon the fire and the gray shapes crept away to the edge of the light, and in the morning they were gone.

It was gray before the dawn and there was a thin frost on the leaves, and he saddled up and started out again, slowly, after the track and into the wind. At sunrise he came upon the ridge of the mountain. For hours he followed the ridge, and he could see for miles across the land. It was late in the autumn and clear, and the great shining slopes, green and blue, rose out of the shadows on either side, and the sunlit groves of aspen shone bright with clusters of yellow leaves and thin white lines of bark, and far below in the deep folds of the land he could see the tops of the black pines swaying. At midmorning he was low in a saddle of the ridge, and he came upon a huge outcrop of rock and the track was lost. An ancient watercourse fell away like a flight of stairs to the left, the falls broad and shallow at first, but ever more narrow and deep farther down. He tied the horses and started down the rock on foot, using the rifle to balance himself. He went slowly, quietly down until he came to a deep open funnel in the rock. The ground on either side sloped sharply down to a broad ravine and the edge of the timber beyond, and he saw the scored earth where the bear had left the rock and gone sliding down, and the swatch in the brush of the ravine. He thought of going the same way; it would be quick and easy, and he was close to the kill, closing in and growing restless. But he must make no sound of hurry. The bear knew he was coming, knew better than he how close he was, was even now watching him from the wood, waiting, but still he must make no sound of hurry. The walls of the funnel were deep and smooth, and they converged at the bank of the ravine some twenty feet below, and the ravine was filled with sweet clover and paintbrush and sage. He held the rifle out as far as he could reach and let it go; it fell upon a stand of tall sweet clover with scarcely any sound, and the dull stock shone and the long barrel glinted among the curving green and yellow stalks. He let himself down into the funnel, little by little, supported only by the tension of his strength against the walls. The going was hard and slow, and near the end his arms and legs began to shake, but he was young and strong and he dropped from the point of the rock to the sand below and took up the rifle and went on, not hurrying but going only as fast as the bear had gone, going even in the bear's tracks, across the ravine and up the embankment and through the trees, unwary now, sensible only of closing in, going on and looking down at the tracks.

And when at last he looked up, the timber around a pool of light, and the bear was standing still and small at the far side of the brake, careless, unheeding. He brought the rifle up, and the bear raised and turned its head and made no sign of fear. It was small and black in the deep shade and dappled with light, its body turned three-quarters away and standing perfectly still, and the flat head and the small black eyes that were fixed upon him hung around upon the shoulder and under the hump of the spine. The bear was young and heavy with tallow, and the underside of the body and the backs of its short, thick legs were tufted with winter hair, longer and lighter than the rest, and dull as dust. His hand tightened on the stock and the rifle bucked and the sharp report rang upon the walls and carried out upon the slopes, and he heard the sudden scattering of birds overhead and saw the darting shadows all around. The bullet slammed into the flesh and jarred the whole black body once, but the head remained motionless and the eyes level upon him. Then, and for one instant only, there was a sad and meaningless haste. The bear turned away and lumbered, though not with fear, not with any hurt, but haste, slightly reflexive, and a single step, or two, or three, and it was overcome. It shuddered and looked around again and fell.

The hunt was over, and only then could he hurry; it was over and well done. The wound was small and clean, behind the foreleg and low on the body, where the fur and flesh were thin, and there was no blood at the mouth. He took out his pouch of pollen and made yellow streaks above the bear's eyes. It was almost noon, and he hurried. He disemboweled the bear and laid the flesh open with splints so that the blood should not run into the fur and stain the hide. He ate quickly of the bear's liver, taking it with him, thinking what he must do, remembering now his descent upon the rock and the whole lay of the land, all the angles of his vision from the ridge. He went quickly, a quarter of a mile or more down the ravine, until he came to a place where the horses could keep their footing on the near side of the ridge. The blood of the bear was on him, and the bear's liver was warm and wet in his hand. He came upon the ridge and the colt grew wild in its eyes and blew, pulling away, and its hoofs clattered on the rock and the skin crawled at the roots of its mane. He approached it slowly, talking to it, and took hold of the reins. The hunting horse watched, full of age and indifference, switching its tail. There was no time to lose. He held hard to the reins, turning down the bit in the colt's mouth, and his voice rose a little and was edged. Slowly he brought the bear's flesh up to the flaring nostrils of the colt and smeared the muzzle with it.

As he rode the colt back down the mountain, leading the hunting horse with the bear on its back, and, like the old hunting horse and the young black bear, he and the colt had come of age and were hunters, too. He made camp that night far down in the peneplain and saw the stars and heard the coyotes away by the river. And in the early morning he rode into the town. He was a man then, and smeared with the blood of a bear. He shouted, and the men came out to meet him. They came with rifles, and he gave them strips of the bear's flesh, which they wrapped around the barrels of their guns. And soon the women came with switches, and they spoke to the bear and laid the switches to its hide. The men and women were jubilant and all around, and he rode stone-faced in their midst, looking straight ahead. . . .

2

FROM

Black Elk Speaks

by Black Elk
as told through John G. Neihardt

A tale of love thwarted and finally triumphant becomes a favorite story of all peoples. The following story of the courtship of High Horse, a young Oglala Sioux, makes a delightful addition to the literature of love. Tempered by a gentle humor, the story captures the passion of a young Indian man for a beautiful woman.

Among many Indian tribes it was traditional for the young men to court women at night. It was equally traditional for them not to get caught while doing so. Suspicious parents had to be eluded or outwitted, as High Horse painfully learned.

Though the trials High Horse endured in order to gain his wife were torturous for him, they were not without reason. As in all cultures, the young woman's father wanted the assurance of a worthy husband for his daughter.

You know, in the old days, it was not so very easy to get a girl when you wanted to be married. Sometimes it was hard work for a young man and he had to stand a great deal. Say I am a young man and I have seen a young girl who looks so beautiful to me that I feel all sick when I think about her. I can not just go and tell her about it and then get married if she is willing. I have to be a very sneaky fellow to talk to her at all, and after I have managed to talk to her, that is only the beginning.

Probably for a long time I have been feeling sick about a certain girl because I love her so much, but she will not even look at me, and her parents keep a good watch over her. But I keep feeling worse and worse all the time; so maybe I sneak up to her tepee in the dark and wait until she comes out. Maybe I just wait there all night and don't get any sleep at all and she does not come out. Then I feel sicker than ever about her.

Maybe I hide in the brush by a spring where she sometimes goes to get water, and when she comes by, if nobody is looking, then I jump out and hold her and just make her listen to me. If she likes me too, I can tell that from the way she acts, for she is very bashful and maybe will not say a word or even look at me the first time. So I let her go, and then maybe I sneak around until I can see her father alone, and tell him how many horses I can give him for his beautiful girl, and by now I am feeling so sick that maybe I would give him all the horses in the world if I had them.

Well, this young man I am telling about was called High Horse, and there was a girl in the village who looked so beautiful to him that he was just sick all over from thinking about her so much and he was getting sicker all the time. The girl was very shy, and her parents thought a great deal of her because they were not young any more and this was the only child they had. So they watched her all day long, and they fixed it so that she would be safe at night too when they were asleep. They thought so much of her that they had made a rawhide bed for her to sleep in, and after they knew that High Horse was sneaking around after her, they took rawhide thongs and tied the girl in bed at night so that nobody could steal her when they were asleep, for they were not sure but that their girl might really want to be stolen.

Well, after High Horse had been sneaking around a good while and hiding and waiting for the girl and getting sicker all the time, he finally caught her alone and made her talk to him. Then he found out that she liked him maybe a little.

Of course this did not make him feel well. It made him sicker than ever, but now he felt as brave as a bison bull, and so he went right to her father and said he loved the girl so much that he would give two good horses for her—one of them young and the other one not so very old.

But the old man just waved his hand, meaning for High Horse to go away and quit talking foolishness like that.

High Horse was feeling sicker than ever about it; but there was another young fellow who said he would loan High Horse two ponies and when he got some more horses, why, he could just give them back for the ones he had borrowed.

Then High Horse went back to the old man and said he would give four horses for the girl—two of them young and the other two not hardly old at all. But the old man just waved his hand and would not say anything.

So High Horse sneaked around until he could talk to the girl again, and he asked her to run away with him. He told her he thought he would just fall over and die if she did not. But she said she would not do that; she wanted to be bought like a fine woman. You see she thought a great deal of herself too.

That made High Horse feel so very sick that he could not eat a bite, and he went around with his head hanging down as though he might just fall down and die any time.

Red Deer was another young fellow, and he and High Horse were great comrades, always doing things together. Red Deer saw how High Horse was acting, and he said: "Cousin, what is the matter? Are you sick in the belly? You look as though you were going to die."

Then High Horse told Red Deer how it was, and said he thought he could not stay alive much longer if he could not marry the girl pretty quick.

Red Deer thought awhile about it, and then he said: "Cousin, I have a plan, and if you are man enough to do as I tell you, then everything will be all right. She will not run away with you; her old man will not take four horses; and four horses are all you can get. You must steal her and run away with her. Then afterwhile you can come back and the old man cannot do anything because she will be your woman. Probably she wants you to steal her anyway."

So they planned what High Horse had to do, and he said he loved the girl so much that he was man enough to do anything Red Deer or anybody else could think up.

So this is what they did.

That night late they sneaked up to the girl's tepee and waited until it sounded inside as though the old man and the old woman and the girl were sound asleep. Then High Horse crawled under the tepee with a knife. He had to cut the rawhide thongs first, and then Red Deer, who was pulling up the stakes around that side of the tepee, was going to help drag the girl outside and gag her. After that, High Horse could put her across his pony in front of him and hurry out of there and be happy all the rest of his life.

When High Horse had crawled inside, he felt so nervous that he could hear his heart drumming, and it seemed so loud he felt sure it would 'waken the old folks. But it did not, and afterwhile he began cutting the thongs. Every time he cut one it made a pop and nearly scared him to death. But he was getting along all right and all the thongs were cut down as far as the girl's thighs, when he became so nervous that his knife slipped and stuck the girl. She gave a big, loud yell. Then the old folks jumped up and yelled too. By this time High Horse was outside, and he and Red Deer were running away like antelope. The old man and some other people chased the young men but they got away in the dark and nobody knew who it was.

Well, if you ever wanted a beautiful girl you will know how sick High Horse was now. It was very bad the way he felt, and it looked as though he would starve even if he did not drop over dead sometime.

Red Deer kept thinking about this, and after a few days he went to High Horse and said: "Cousin, take courage! I have another plan, and I am sure, if you are man enough, we can steal her this time." And High Horse said: "I am man enough to do anything anybody can think up, if I can only get that girl."

So this is what they did.

They went away from the village alone, and Red Deer made High Horse strip naked. Then he painted High Horse solid white all over, and after that he painted black stripes all over the white and put black rings around High Horse's eyes. High Horse looked terrible. He looked so terrible that when Red Deer was through painting and took a good look at what he had done, he said it scared even him a little.

"Now," Red Deer said, "if you get caught again, everybody will be so scared they will think you are a bad spirit and will be afraid to chase you."

So when the night was getting old and everybody was sound asleep, they sneaked back to the girl's tepee. High Horse crawled in with his knife, as before, and Red Deer waited outside, ready to drag the girl out and gag her when High Horse had all the thongs cut.

High Horse crept up by the girl's bed and began cutting at the thongs. But he kept thinking, "If they see me they will shoot me because I look so terrible." The girl was restless and kept squirming around in bed, and when a thong was cut, it popped. So High Horse worked very slowly and carefully.

But he must have made some noise, for suddenly the old woman awoke and said to her old man: "Old Man, wake up! There is somebody in the tepee!" But the old man was sleepy and didn't want to be bothered. He said: "Of course there is somebody in this tepee. Go to sleep and don't bother me." Then he snored some more.

But High Horse was so scared by now that he lay very still and as flat to the ground as he could. Now, you see, he had not been sleeping very well for a long time because he was so sick about the girl. And while he was lying there waiting for the old woman to snore, he just forgot everything, even how beautiful the girl was. Red Deer who was lying outside ready to do his part, wondered and wondered what had happened in there, but he did not dare call out to High Horse.

Afterwhile the day began to break and Red Deer had to leave with the two ponies he had staked there for his comrade and girl, or somebody would see him.

So he left.

Now when it was getting light in the tepee, the girl awoke and the first thing she saw was a terrible animal, all white with black stripes on it, lying asleep beside her bed. So she screamed, and then the old woman screamed and the old man yelled. High Horse jumped up, scared almost to death, and he nearly knocked the tepee down getting out of there.

People were coming running from all over the village with guns and bows and axes, and everybody was yelling.

By now High Horse was running so fast that he hardly touched the ground at all, and he looked so terrible that the people fled from him and let him run. Some braves wanted to shoot at him, but the others said he might be some sacred being and it would bring bad trouble to kill him.

High Horse made for the river that was near, and in among the brush he found a hollow tree and dived into it. After-while some braves came there and he could hear them saying that it was some bad spirit that had come out of the water and gone back in again.

That morning the people were ordered to break camp and move away from there. So they did, while High Horse was hiding in his hollow tree.

Now Red Deer had been watching all this from his own tepee and trying to look as though he were as much surprised and scared as all the others. So when the camp moved, he sneaked back to where he had seen his comrade disappear. When he was down there in the brush, he called, and High Horse answered, because he knew his friend's voice. They washed off the paint from High Horse and sat down on the river bank to talk about their troubles.

High Horse said he never would go back to the village as long as he lived and he did not care what happened to him now. He said he was going to go on the war-path all by himself. Red Deer said: "No, cousin, you are not going on the war-path alone, because I am going with you."

So Red Deer got everything ready, and at night they started out on the war-path all alone. After several days they came to a Crow camp just about sundown, and when it was dark they sneaked up to where the Crow horses were grazing, killed the horse guard, who was not thinking about enemies because he thought all the Lakotas were far away, and drove off about a hundred horses.

They got a big start because all the Crow horses stampeded and it was probably morning before the Crow warriors could catch any horses to ride. Red Deer and High Horse fled with their herd three days and nights before they reached the village of their people. Then they drove the whole herd right into the village and up in front of the girl's tepee. The old man was there, and High Horse called out to him and asked if he thought maybe that would be enough horses for his girl. The old man did not wave him away that time. It was not the horses that he wanted. What he wanted was a son who was a real man and good for something.

So High Horse got his girl after all, and I think he deserved her.

3

Love Song (Chippewa)

Anonymous

The songs of the Chippewa tribes of northern Wisconsin and Minnesota are beautiful in their simplicity. Concise and compact, these songs often imply more than they say, leaving much to the listener's imagination. In the original musical form melody and rhythm contributed as much as the words to convey the meaning of the song.

According to Frances Densmore, the most knowledgeable twentieth-century commentator on Indian songs, the love song is a modern development among the Chippewa. The choice of love as thematic material has been greatly influenced by contact with white civilization.

> Oh
> I am thinking
> Oh
> I am thinking
> I have found
> my lover
> Oh I think it is so.
>
> To a very distant land
> he is going
> my lover
> soon
> he will come again.

4

FROM

Sketch of the Eventful Life of Okah Tubbee

by Okah Tubbee

On his second voyage to the New World, Christopher Columbus imposed slavery upon the aboriginal inhabitants of the land. He forcibly subdued the natives of the island of Española and enslaved every Indian over the age of fourteen. In 1494, Columbus sent over 500 natives to be sold in Spain. Exposed to the rigors of a life of servitude and weakened by exposure to European diseases, the native population of the West Indies could not survive. Many Indians committed suicide, and women refused to bear children. Within thirty years the number of natives in the West Indies was greatly reduced.

This pattern followed wherever the Spanish settled. Florida and the southern United States became a source for Spanish slave raiders from 1500 to 1550. Spaniards also found victims in Mexico and the southwestern United States. In the Southwest, native American tribes were induced to capture and trade members of enemy tribes to the Spanish.

During the American colonial period Indian slavery was widespread in New England and in the South. South Carolina held the greatest number of Indian slaves at that time. In 1708 the total population of South Carolina was 9,580. Of this number, 2,900 were black slaves and 1,400 were Indian slaves.

The following selection is part of an account of the life of an American Indian slave. Okah Tubbee was taken from his Choctaw family as a young boy and placed by a white master in the home of a black slave woman. There he was abused and beaten by his new "mother." In his autobiographical sketch Okah Tubbee relates the story of his first encounter with Indians in Natchez, Mississippi, and the joyous rediscovery of his Indian heritage.

As a young man Tubbee gained his freedom and embarked upon a career of missionary work among the Indians of the eastern United States. This narrative was published by the author in 1848.

The first recollections of my childhood are scenes of sorrow; though I have an imperfect recollection of a kind father, who was a very large man, with dark red skin, and his head was adorned with feathers of a most beautiful plumage. I seem to have been happy then, and remember the green woods, and that he took me out at night, and taught me to look up to the stars, and said many things to me that made my young heart swell with sweet hope, as it filled with thoughts too large for it to retain. This scene soon changed, for I had a new father, or a man who took me to a new home, which proves to have been Natchez, Mississippi. I have no recollection where this intercourse took place with my own father, but from various circumstances which have since occurred, I am led to believe that it must have been upon the Dancing Rabbit Creek, (Tombigbee) before the Choctaws removed from their old homes. I soon found this was not my own father, neither in appearance nor in action, and began to understand that I could have but one father. This man was white, and a slave woman had the management of his house; she had two children, who were older than myself, a boy and a girl; she was very fond of them, but was never even kind to me, yet they obliged me to call her mother. I was always made to serve the two children, though many times I had to be whipped into obedience. If I had permission to go out an hour to play I chose to be alone, that I might weep over my situation; but even this consolation was refused me. I was forced to go in company with them, taking with me, many times, a smarting back, after a promise had been extorted from me that I would remain with them and obey them. I soon found myself boxing heartily with the boys, both white and black, because they called me nigger, and everything but that which was true, for I could not and would not submit to such gross insults without defending myself, which is so characteristic of the red man. Her children were well dressed and neat; I was not only in rags, but many times my proud heart seemed crushed within me, and my cheek crimsoned with shame because of their filthy condition, and I often left them off in consequence, but soon learned to take them off and wash them myself, such was my abhorrence of filth. I was compelled to go in a naked state to enable me to wash my clothes, and they upbraided me for my nakedness, but I replied, where did you ever see or hear of a child being born with clothes on? I was then a child too young to work, but did errands. . . .

I gave the woman my money, also the presents I received, but the more I gave her, the more she exacted from me. Child as I was, I could not allow myself to weep by day. If she found my pillow wet with my tears, she whipped me for that and I formed a habit of going alone at night, and lifting my heart to God in prayer, for his preservation, and that my father might return. When I stood thus alone, in the open air, a feeling of hope was within my heart, as I felt thus alone before God, with the stars, which in my childish language I called the eyes of heaven, gazing down upon me; here I gained fortitude to bear all my wrongs—here I determined to ask the white man, whom I sometimes saw, about my own father. I had now and then mentioned it to the woman, she always told with tongue and heart, begone! outlandish savage, you never had any father. As she was always angry at my inclination to be alone about this time, she gave me a severe whipping for climbing a bluff which no other boy dared to, and thus spending a Sabbath with my thoughts, tears, prayers, and childish aspirations. The point was called Buzzard Roost.

I have since thought she in her anger, forgot herself at this time, for she asked me if I did not know that this was the way Indians and all wild savages lived, and could not be tamed—that the white people could not make as much service of them, as they could of the blacks for they would not work for them, but spent their lives wandering about in the woods, both day and night, living with the wild beasts. Now I loved wild beasts, and my heart was swelling within me; I forgot her evil blows as with clasped hands, and tearful eyes, my heart kindled with the most intense emotion at her recital. I cried out, Oh! tell me more, tell me more. She looked at me, said something about the strange wild light in my eyes— seated herself, and seemed in deep thought. She then said something which I did not understand, though I listened, for I thought she was going to tell me more. I think she said in a soliloquy, 'what is bred in the bone will be in the marrow,' consequently, when I hear the remark, my mind resorts to this scene of my childhood, with peculiar emotion, and intense interest. I accordingly asked the white man where he found me, and when my father would come for me. He seemed astonished to find I had any recollection of a father before I saw him. He told me I had been dreaming that he was not my father; bade me remember I was this woman's child, and she could do as she pleased with me; bade me never to mention this thing to any one, nor speak of it again to him; but told me I would know more about it, when old enough to work. Here I gave myself up to despair. . . .

One day I walked down to the river, and found Steam Boats from every part of the great valley of the Mississippi. The captain of one of them, bound to Red River, who knew I was unprotected, and without employment, asked how I would like a trip to Alexandria, saying he thought it would improve my health and spirits. I told him if I could pay my expenses I would gladly go. I was soon on board, and the boat under way. Before we reached the place of destination, I frankly told the Captain my belief respecting my birth, and that I did not wish to return, but rather to remain in that country to visit some of the Indian villages—he willingly permitted me to stay, and promised to say nothing on his return respecting my retreat. I here felt reassured, and though I had no friends present, it was a comfort to know I had no enemies. I soon obtained sundry small jobs, which paid for my board, and something besides. I did not wish to enter into steady employment, as I intended the first opportunity to visit the Indians.

Perhaps I should have stated, that I had seen Indians frequently in Natchez, but soon learned that when any of them came to town, I was carefully and closely watched. It appears that some one always gave the necessary information to whoever I lived with, saying I had threatened to run away with them. Permit me to describe my feelings the first time I ever saw Indians. I had just stepped out of a door into the street as they were coming down the street; they were walking slowly, seeming to be looking at the buildings; I appeared nailed to the spot, my heart leaped with joy, yet a choking sensation amounting to pain seized me; confused ideas crowded upon my mind; they were near me, yet I moved not, until the keen eyes of one of them rested upon me, and then upon each other, while as it seemed to me they uttered an exclamation of surprise; they came towards me; I was wild with delight, I thought I was their child, that they were seeking for me; I started and held out my hands, tears gushed from my eyes, I addressed them in a language to me unknown before; it was neither English, Spanish, or French; astonished they spoke kind to me, smoothing my hair with their hands; an explanation now took place, as one could speak English; he said I had asked in Choctaw for my father, saying that he had gone and left me, and I was with bad people; that I begged to know if he was not with them. They then asked for my mother. This pained me; I told them she was not my mother; they looked at each other, spoke faster and louder, and looked very angry; there had a crowd of children, and men and women gathered; the Indians loudly asked where and to whom does this child belong? Some one answered to a colored woman. The clouds seemed to grow darker on their way, yet to me, sweet fact, the same one said, to a slave woman, and he is a slave. The Indian held his hands high above his head and said 'but white man lie, he no good, him no slave, no nigger, no bad white man steal him, his skin is red;' this was repeated in imperfect English by them all—me I love him—in the crowd were some smoking, laughing, some mocking, angry and cursing. The Indians conversed in a low tone together: here some of the crowd interfered, and separated me from my new, but dear friends—while, all the time, 'bad white man lie, he steal him, he no nigger, him Indian boy,' now and then reached my ears. I was then torn from them. My feelings towards them I cannot attempt to explain.

I here learned that the Indians often visited the village, that they came here and fished, and sold their fish to the inhabitants, and I determined to make their acquaintance here, and so get an invitation to their camps. As I still retained a love for the hook and line, it was just in my hand. The first Indian I met assisted me in a friendly manner, which I returned, and was soon happy among them, for they seemed to regard me as a companion; they did not even ask for or look for other blood in me. I tasked my memory in bringing to mind words, often on my tongue though I had no recollection of their meaning. They told me it was the Choctaw tongue. I was over anxious to gain the friendship of those who spoke a little English, and as soon as I was sure of their confidence, I gave to them a history of my sorrows in part; it was night, and we were gathered around the camp fire, one of them serving as interpreter. I had scarcely begun before the pipe was laid by, one saying their hearts were sorry, and they could not smoke; the elder ones bent their eyes on the ground, their features settled into an immovable silence, their arms were folded upon their breasts; their very silence said to me; this is but another lesson in the deceitfulness of the pale face. The eyes of the younger ones were fixed upon me, and their features manifested a restlessness, and they manifested signs of revenge; they grasped their tomahawks firmly; my emotion soon prevented my proceeding. I showed them my back [marked with scars from frequent beatings]; that expression, eagh! eagh! eagh! so significant of high resolves, contempt, and indignation, &c., escaped the lips of the older, while an angry wail went forth from the young. Their leader spoke when all was silent; their interpreter gave me what follows: 'Pale face always say he friend, poor Indian got no money, bad pale face get fire-water, then he friend; Indian got no money, then he got no friend; but he got hunting-ground, pale face want it, he fight a little, give little this, and little that, last poor Indian take fire-water, he then loses sense, then white man get his home. The Great Spirit gave pale face children, houses, cattle, but this not enough; he think Indian make good slave, so he try him; but he no make slave; so bad white man steal papoose, may be he make good slave. No, no, no, bad white man, he no good, he speak with a forked tongue.' While he was speaking not a motion was made or any other sound heard; not a leaf trembled; as he ceased my ears were almost deafened with the loud yells of indignation that burst upon me as they sprang to their feet and began dancing around me. This was a scene novel to me; I had roused their feelings for me, but knew not how to quiet them.

It was late before we laid down in our wigwams; we arose very early; they said they could not sleep and were sorry for their brother's son, and their fears plainly showed that they were ill at ease. We washed ourselves all over, thoroughly; they gathered around the fire, standing in a circle, holding their left hand up to the Great Spirit; said a few words in their own tongue deeply serious, wet the fore finger with the same hand, dipped it in the ashes, beginning at the corner of the eye drew it downwards, imitating the trickling of a tear; their leader then spoke a few words, the others imitating him, at holding up the same hand, their eyes fixed on the morning sky as their words fell from their lips. They looked upon me as though they were reading my heart, instead of searching my features. I did not know how to act, but the interpreter told me they were invoking the Great Spirit for me, and expressing sorrow for my situation. They then very gravely informed me that I must not fish for them any more, as I had caught more fish than they, and they were convinced that the Great Spirit had given me this as a gift to supply my wants, and he would be angry with them if they accepted of any which I could sell. To this I undertook to object, telling them I had some little money and was their visitor, and had partaken of their bread, but still they answered, we also have partaken of your fish. My interpreter here motioned me to be silent; they believed a supernatural power would uphold me, and that these difficulties were suffered to gather around the path to test my honor; that the God of the pale face, and the bad alike, had come before me; if I chose the good, the Great Spirit would deliver me; I then wished to be cheerful, but as long as they let the ashes stay upon their faces, I scarcely spoke; but when this was taken off, I felt at liberty, and attempted to amuse them by telling anecdotes about myself which pleased them so much that they had a great pow-wow about it, and they were in perfect ecstacies about them. . . .

5

Autobiographical Sketch

by John Rollin

As early as 1790 the Cherokee tribe began to adopt the tech-nological innovations of the white man, using tools and implements procured from the United States Government in return for land. They hoped that the emulation of some aspects of white culture would cause the government to rec-ognize them as a civilized people, and thus allow them to remain in their home, the mountain area where Georgia, Tennessee, and North Carolina meet.

In 1821, Sequoya invented an alphabet for the Cherokee language. By 1826 the Cherokee Nation possessed large herds of domesticated animals and had built looms, spinning wheels, saw mills, grist mills, blacksmith shops, cotton machines, eighteen schools, eighteen ferries, and a number of roads. In 1827 the Cherokees adopted a written constitution which established an executive branch of government, a bicameral legislature, a supreme court, and a system of laws.

At this time the Cherokee people petitioned the U.S. Su-preme Court for recognition as a self-governing people. The Court, under Chief Justice John Marshall, upheld their plea against the State of Georgia which had wished to rule the Cherokee Nation. However, emulation of and cooperation with the whites did not secure for the Cherokees their human rights. President Andrew Jackson refused to honor the Su-

*preme Court's decision. Under Jackson's insistence the Con-
gress passed the Indian Removal Act of 1830. The Cherokees
and other tribes of the southeast and northwest were mili-
tarily forced to move to the wilderness west of the Mississippi
River.*

*This removal was expedited by the discovery of gold within
the Indians' Appalachian territory in 1837. The U.S. Army
rounded up the Cherokees into prison camps and then
forcibly marched them westward. During this harsh winter
trip one-quarter of the Cherokees died, and the march became known as "The Trail of Tears."*

*John Rollin, author of the following autobiographical
selection, was the son and grandson of Cherokee leaders. His
family had adopted the white culture; his mother was a white
woman. For him the move west led to personal as well as
tribal tragedy. Divisions arose within the Cherokee Nation
after they had been relocated. Unable to vent their anger
against the whites, the Cherokees turned upon their own
chiefs. John Rollin became a witness to his father's assassination at the hands of his own people.*

I was born in the Cherokee Nation, East of the Mississippi
River, on the 19th of March, 1827. My earliest recollections
are of such things as are pleasing to childhood, the fondness
of a kind father, and smiles of an affectionate mother. My
father, the late John Ridge, as you know, was one of the
Chiefs of his tribe, and son of the warrior and orator dis-
tinguished in Cherokee Councils and battles, who was known
amongst the whites as Major Ridge, and amongst his own
people as Ka-nun-ta-cla-ge. My father grew up till he was
some twelve or fifteen years of age, as any untutored Indian,
and he used well to remember the time when his greatest
delight was to strip himself of his Indian costume, and with
aboriginal cane-gig in hand, while away the long summer
days in wading up and down creeks in search of crawfish.

At the age which I have mentioned above, a missionary
station sprang into existence, and Major Ridge sent his son
John, who could not speak a word of English, to school at

this station, placing him under the instruction of a venerable Missionary named Gambol. Here he learned rapidly, and in the course of a year acquired a sufficient knowledge of the white man's language to speak it quite fluently.

Major Ridge had now become fully impressed with the importance of civilization. He had built him a log-cabin, in imitation of the border-whites, and opened him a farm. The Missionary, Gambol, told him of an institution built up in a distant land expressly for the education of Indian youths (Cornwall, Connecticut), and here he concluded to send his son. After hearing some stern advice from his father, with respect to the manner in which he should conduct himself amongst the "pale-faces," he departed for the "Cornwall School" in charge of a friendly Missionary. He remained there until his education was completed. During his attendance at this institution, he fell in love with a young white girl of the place, daughter of Mr. Northrup. His love was reciprocated. He returned home to his father, gained his consent, though with much difficulty (for the old Major wished him to marry a chief's daughter amongst his own people), went back again to Cornwall, and shortly brought his "pale-face" bride to the wild country of the Cherokees. In due course of time, I, John Rollin, came into the world. I was called by my grandfather "Chees-quat-a-law-ny," which, interpreted, means "Yellow Bird." Thus you have a knowledge of my parentage and how it happened that I am an Indian.

Things had now changed with the Cherokees. They had a written Constitution and laws. They had legislative halls, houses and farms, courts and juries. The general mass, it is true, were ignorant, but happy under the administration of a few simple, just, and wholesome laws. Major Ridge had become wealthy by trading with the whites and by prudent management. He had built him an elegant house on the banks of the "Oos-te-nar-ly River," on which now stands the thriving town of Rome, Georgia. Many a time in my buoyant boyhood have I strayed along its summer-shaded shores, and glided in the light canoe over its swiftly-rolling bosom, and beneath its over-hanging willows. Alas for the beautiful scene! The Indian's form haunts it no more!

My father's residence was a few miles east of the "Oos-te-nar-ly." I remember it well. A large two-storied house, on a high hill, crowned with a fine grove of oak and hickory, a large, clear spring at the foot of the hill, and an extensive farm stretching away down into the valley, with a fine orchard on the left. On another hill some two hundred yards distant, stood the school-house, built at my father's expense, for the use of a Missionary, Miss Sophia Sawyer, who made her home with our family and taught my father's children and all who chose to come for her instruction. I went to this school until I was ten years of age—which was in 1837. Then another change had come over the Cherokee Nation. A demon-spell had fallen upon it. The white man had become covetous of the soil. The unhappy Indian was driven from his house—not one, but thousands—and the white man's ploughshare turned up the acres which he had called his own. Wherever the Indian built his cabin, and planted his corn, there was the spot which the white man craved. Convicted on suspicion, they were sentenced to death by laws whose authority they could not acknowledge, and hanged on the white man's gallows. Oppression became intolerable, and forced by extreme necessity, they at last gave up their homes, yielded their beloved country to the rapacity of the Georgians, and wended their way in silence and in sorrow to the forests of the far west. In 1837, my father moved his family to his new home. He built his houses and opened his farm; gave encouragement to the rising neighborhood, and fed many a hungry and naked Indian whom oppression had prostrated to the dust. A second time he built a school-house, and Miss Sawyer again instructed his own children and the children of his neighbors. Two years rolled away in quietude, but the Spring of '39 brought in a terrible train of events. Parties had arisen in the Nation. The removal West had fomented discontents of the darkest and deadliest nature. The ignorant Indians, unable to vent their rage on the whites, turned their wrath towards their own chiefs, and chose to hold them responsible for what had happened. John Ross made use of these prejudices to establish his own power. He held a secret council and plotted the death of my father and grandfather, and Boudinot, and others, who were friendly to the interests of these men. John Ridge was at this time the most powerful man in the Nation, and it was necessary for Ross, in order to realize his ambitious scheme for ruling the whole Nation, not only to put the Ridges out of the way, but those who most prominently supported them, lest they might cause trouble afterwards. These bloody deeds were perpetrated under circumstances of peculiar aggravation. On the morning of the 22d of June, 1839, about day-break, our family was aroused from sleep by a violent noise. The doors were broken down, and the house was full of armed men. I saw my father in the hands of assassins. He endeavored to speak to them, but they shouted and drowned his voice, for they were instructed not to listen to him for a moment, for fear they would be persuaded not to kill him. They dragged him into the yard, and prepared to murder him. Two men held him by the arms, and others by the body, while another stabbed him deliberately with a dirk twenty-nine times. My mother rushed out to the door, but they pushed her back with their guns into the house, and prevented her egress until their act was finished, when they left the place quietly. My father fell to the earth, but did not immediately expire. My mother ran out to him. He raised himself on his elbow and tried to speak, but the blood flowed into his mouth and prevented him. In a few moments more he died, without speaking that last word which he wished to say. Then succeeded a scene of agony the sight of which might make one regret that the human race had ever been created. It has darkened my mind with an eternal shadow. In a room prepared for the purpose, lay pale in death the man whose voice had been listened to with awe and admiration in the councils of his Nation, and whose fame had passed to the remotest of the United States, the blood oozing through his winding sheet, and falling drop by drop on the floor. By his side sat my mother, with hands clasped, and in speechless agony—she who had given him her heart in the days of her youth and beauty, left the home of her parents, and followed the husband of her choice to a wild and distant land. And bending over him was his own afflicted mother, with her long, white hair flung loose over her shoulders and bosom, crying to the Great Spirit to sustain her in that dreadful hour. And in addition to all these, the wife, the mother and the little children, who scarcely knew their loss, were the dark faces of those who had been the murdered man's friends, and, possibly, some who had been privy to the assassination, who had come to smile over the scene.

There was yet another blow to be dealt. Major Ridge had started on a journey the day before to Van Buren, a town on the Arkansas River, in the State of Arkansas. He was traveling down what was called the Line Road, in the direction of Evansville. A runner was sent with all possible speed to inform him of what had happened. The runner returned with the news that Major Ridge himself was killed. It is useless to lengthen description. It would fall short, far short of the theme.

These events happened when I was twelve years old. Great excitement existed in the Nation, and my mother thinking her children unsafe in the country of their father's murderers, and unwilling to remain longer where all that she saw reminded her of her dreadful bereavement, removed to the State of Arkansas, and settled in the town of Fayettville. In that place I went to school till I was fourteen years of age, when my mother sent me to New England to finish my education. . . .

I shall not return to the Nation now until circumstances are materially changed. I shall cast my fortunes for some years with the whites. I am twenty-three years old, married, and have an infant daughter. I will still devote my life to my people, though not amongst them, and before I die, I hope to see the Cherokee Nation, in conjunction with the Choctaws, admitted into the Confederacy of the United States.

6

FROM

Black Elk Speaks

by Black Elk
as told through John G. Neihardt

*Black Elk, a holy man of the Oglala Sioux, painfully wit-
nessed the destruction of his people. As a boy of nine he
experienced a powerful vision. According to this vision he
was to become a leader of his people, healing the nation,
leading it through times of adversity to a flowering rebirth.
In the dream, the Sioux people appeared to Black Elk as a
hoop. The spiritual grandfathers of the vision gave to Black
Elk a holy stick, instructing him to set it in the center of
the hoop where it would grow into "a shielding tree and
bloom."*

*The course of Black Elk's life was determined by this early
vision. He lived among his people as a medicine man until
he was twenty-three. By then, in 1886, the Oglala were in
despair. Their homes in the sacred Black Hills were taken
from them by whites who had discovered gold there. At this
time Black Elk decided to travel across the big water (the
Atlantic) in order to learn some secret of the white man which
might help the Sioux. In the following selection he relates
his experiences during this period when he traveled with a
Wild West show to England.*

. . . I can remember when the bison were so many that they
could not be counted, but more and more Wasichus [white

men] came to kill them until there were only heaps of bones scattered where they used to be. The Wasichus did not kill them to eat; they killed them for the metal that makes them crazy, and they took only the hides to sell. Sometimes they did not even take the hides, only the tongues; and I have heard that fire-boats came down the Missouri River loaded with dried bison tongues. You can see that the men who did this were crazy. Sometimes they did not even take the tongues; they just killed and killed because they liked to do that. When we hunted bison, we killed only what we needed. And when there was nothing left but heaps of bones, the Wasichus came and gathered up even the bones and sold them.

All our people now were settling down in square gray houses, scattered here and there across this hungry land, and around them the Wasichus had drawn a line to keep them in. The nation's hoop was broken, and there was no center any longer for the flowering tree. The people were in despair. They seemed heavy to me, heavy and dark; so heavy that it seemed they could not be lifted; so dark that they could not be made to see any more. Hunger was among us often now, for much of what the Great Father in Washington sent us must have been stolen by Wasichus who were crazy to get money. There were many lies, but we could not eat them. The forked tongue made promises.

I kept on curing the sick for three years more, and many came to me and were made over; but when I thought of my great vision, which was to save the nation's hoop and make the holy tree to bloom in the center of it, I felt like crying, for the sacred hoop was broken and scattered. The life of the people was in the hoop, and what are many little lives if the life of those lives be gone?

But late in my twenty-third summer (1886), it seemed that there was a little hope. There came to us some Wasichus who wanted a band of Oglalas for a big show that the other Pahuska ["Long Hair" Buffalo Bill] had. They told us this show would go across the big water to strange lands, and I thought I ought to go, because I might learn some secret of the Wasichu that would help my people somehow. In my great vision, when I stood at the center of the world, the two men from the east had brought me the daybreak-star herb and they had told me to drop it on the earth; and where it touched the ground it took root and bloomed four-rayed. It was the herb of understanding. Also, where the red man of my vision changed into a bison that rolled, the same herb grew and bloomed when the bison had vanished, and after that the people in my vision found the good red road again. Maybe if I could see the great world of the Wasichu, I could understand how to bring the sacred hoop together and make the tree bloom again at the center of it.

I looked back on the past and recalled my people's old ways, but they were not living that way any more. They were traveling the black road, everybody for himself and with little rules of his own, as in my vision. I was in despair, and I even thought that if the Wasichus had a better way, then maybe my people should live that way. I know now that this was foolish, but I was young and in despair.

My relatives told me I should stay at home and go on curing people, but I would not listen to them.

The show people sent wagons from Rushville on the iron road to get us, and we were about a hundred men and women. Many of our people followed us half way to the iron road and there we camped and ate together. Afterward we left our people crying there, for we were going very far across the big water.

That evening where the big wagons were waiting for us on the iron road, we had a dance. Then we got into the wagons. When we started, it was dark, and thinking of my home and my people made me very sad. I wanted to get off and run back. But we went roaring all night long, and in the morning we ate at Long Pine. Then we started again and went roaring all day and came to a very big town in the evening [Omaha].

Then we roared along all night again and came to a much bigger town [Chicago]. There we stayed all day and all night; and right there I could compare my people's ways with Wasichu ways, and this made me sadder than before. I wished and wished that I had not gone away from home.

Then we went roaring on again, and afterwhile we came
to a still bigger town—a very big town [New York]. We
walked through this town to the place where the show was
[Madison Square Garden]. Some Pawnees and Omahas were
there, and when they saw us they made war-cries and charged,
couping us. They were doing this for fun and because they
felt glad to see us. I was surprised at the big houses and so
many people, and there were bright lights at night, so that
you could not see the stars, and some of these lights, I heard,
were made with the power of thunder.

We stayed there and made shows for many, many Wasichus
all that winter. I liked the part of the show we made, but not
the part the Wasichus made. Afterwhile I got used to being
there, but I was like a man who had never had a vision. I
felt dead and my people seemed lost and I thought I might
never find them again. I did not see anything to help my
people. I could see that the Wasichus did not care for each
other the way our people did before the nation's hoop was
broken. They would take everything from each other if they
could, and so there were some who had more of everything
than they could use, while crowds of people had nothing at
all and maybe were starving. They had forgotten that the
earth was their mother. This could not be better than the
old ways of my people. There was a prisoner's house on an
island where the big water came up to the town, and we saw
that one day. Men pointed guns at the prisoners and made
them move around like animals in a cage. This made me
feel very sad, because my people too were penned up in
islands, and maybe that was the way the Wasichus were going
to treat them.

In the spring it got warmer, but the Wasichus had even
the grass penned up. We heard then that we were going to
cross the big water to strange lands. Some of our people went
home and wanted me to go with them, but I had not seen
anything good for my people yet; maybe across the big water
there was something to see, so I did not go home, although
I was sick and in despair.

They put us all on a very big fire-boat, so big that when I

first saw it, I could hardly believe it; and when it sent forth a voice, I was frightened. There were other big fire-boats sending voices, and little ones too.

Afterwhile I could see nothing but water, water, water, and we did not seem to be going anywhere, just up and down; but we were told that we were going fast. If we were, I thought that we must drop off where the water ended; or maybe we might have to stop where the sky came down to the water. There was nothing but mist where the big town used to be and nothing but water all around.

We were all in despair now and many were feeling so sick that they began to sing their death-songs.

When evening came, a big wind was roaring and the water thundered. We had things that were meant to be hung up while we slept in them. This I learned afterward. We did not know what to do with these, so we spread them out on the floor and lay down on them. The floor tipped in every direction, and this got worse and worse, so that we rolled from one side to the other and could not sleep. We were frightened, and now we were all very sick too. At first the Wasichus laughed at us; but very soon we could see that they were frightened too, because they were running around and were very much excited. Our women were crying and even some of the men cried, because it was terrible and they could do nothing. Afterwhile the Wasichus came and gave us things to tie around us so that we could float. I did not put on the one they gave me. I did not want to float. Instead, I dressed for death, putting on my best clothes that I wore in the show, and then I sang my death song. Others dressed for death too, and sang, because if it was the end of our lives and we could do nothing, we wanted to die brave. We could not fight this that was going to kill us, but we could die so that our spirit relatives would not be ashamed of us. It was harder for us because we were all so sick. Everything we had eaten came right up, and then it kept on trying to come up when there was nothing there.

We did not sleep at all, and in the morning the water looked like mountains, but the wind was not so strong. Some of the bison and elk that we had with us for the show died that day, and the Wasichus threw them in the water. When I saw the poor bison thrown over, I felt like crying, because I thought right there they were throwing part of the power of my people away.

After we had been on the fire-boat a long while, we could see many houses and then many other fire-boats tied close together along the bank. We thought now we could get off very soon, but we could not. There was a little fire-boat that had come through the gate of waters and it stopped beside us, and the people on it looked at everything on our fire-boat before we could get off. We went very slowly nearly all day, I think, and afterwhile we came to where there were many, many houses close together, and more fire-boats than could be counted. These houses were different from what we had seen before. The Wasichus kept us on the fire-boat all night and then they unloaded us, and took us to a place where the show was going to be. The name of this very big town was London. We were on land now, but we still felt dizzy as though we were still on water, and at first it was hard to walk.

We stayed in this place six moons; and many, many people came to see the show.

One day we were told that Majesty was coming. I did not know what that was at first, but I learned afterward. It was Grandmother England (Queen Victoria), who owned Grandmother's Land where we lived awhile after the Wasichus murdered Crazy Horse.

She came to the show in a big shining wagon, and there were soldiers on both sides of her, and many other shining wagons came too. That day other people could not come to the show—just Grandmother England and some people who came with her.

Sometimes we had to shoot in the show, but this time we did not shoot at all. We danced and sang, and I was one of the dancers chosen to do this for the Grandmother, because I was young and limber then and could dance many ways. We stood right in front of Grandmother England. She was little but fat and we liked her, because she was good to us.

After we had danced, she spoke to us. She said something like this: "I am sixty-seven years old. All over the world I have seen all kinds of people; but to-day I have seen the best-looking people I know. If you belonged to me, I would not let them take you around in a show like this." She said other good things too, and then she said we must come to see her, because she had come to see us. She shook hands with all of us. Her hand was very little and soft. We gave a big cheer for her, and then the shining wagons came in and she got into one of them and they all went away.

In about a half-moon after that we went to see the Grandmother. They put us in some of those shining wagons and took us to a very beautiful place where there was a very big house with sharp, pointed towers on it. There were many seats built high in a circle, and these were just full of Wasichus who were all pounding their heels and yelling: "Jubilee! Jubilee! Jubilee!" I never heard what this meant.

They put us together in a certain place at the bottom of the seats. First there appeared a beautiful black wagon with two black horses, and it went all around the show place. I heard that the Grandmother's grandson, a little boy, was in that wagon. Next came a beautiful black wagon with four gray horses. On each of the two right-hand horses there was a rider, and a man walked, holding the front left-hand horse. I heard that some of Grandmother's relatives were in this wagon. Next came eight buckskin horses, two by two, pulling a shining black wagon. There was a rider on each right-hand horse and a man walked, holding the front left-hand horse. There were soldiers, with bayonets, facing outward all around this wagon. Now all the people in the seats were roaring and yelling "Jubilee!" and "Victoria!" Then we saw Grandmother England again. She was sitting in the back of the wagon and two women sat in the front, facing her. Her dress was all shining and her hat was all shining and her wagon was all shining and so were the horses. She looked like a fire coming.

Afterward I heard that there was yellow and white metal all over the horses and the wagon.

When she came to where we were, her wagon stopped and

she stood up. Then all those people stood up and roared and bowed to her; but she bowed to us. We sent up a great cry and our women made the tremolo. The people in the crowd were so excited that we heard some of them got sick and fell over. Then when it was quiet, we sang a song to the Grandmother.

That was a very happy time.

We liked Grandmother England, because we could see that she was a fine woman, and she was good to us. Maybe if she had been our Grandmother, it would have been better for our people.

II

The Indian Way
of Life

Throughout the history of America's colonization and later development, various stereotypes of the Indian have arisen. The Indian was first seen as a savage, uncivilized in the western manner, and therefore inhumane. Later, in the eighteenth century, romantic writers developed a sentimentalized myth of the Indian as the Noble Savage, a pure and glorious example of man in the natural state. In the nineteenth century, the Indian was again seen as a blood-thirsty, beastly savage, an impediment to the development of an advanced American civilization. Seen in this way, the Indian then became an object to be removed, to be destroyed. In the twentieth century the Indian was regarded as a "problem" in the economic and social development of the country. He once more became an object, this time to be administered, to be shunted through the back doors of government bureaucracies.

Never, however, was the Indian truly known for what he was. White society didn't care to find out the truth; it merely fabricated its own conception of the Indian and treated him in accordance with its own false and derogatory definition.

It is the purpose of the following section to provide a platform from which various American Indians will speak, explaining their own values and philosophies of life.

It is the editors' hope in presenting these selections that the reader will come to recognize the tremendous humanistic values inherent in Indian life. The loss to American society that has occurred through centuries of repression and destruction of Indian culture should not continue.

1

FROM

The Soul of the Indian

by Charles A. Eastman

The laws and customs of American Indian societies were built upon values greatly different from the values of white western society. The accumulation of private property was not a cornerstone of social organization for the Indian. A man was more highly regarded for the wealth he gave away than for the goods he kept. Silence, as well as generosity, was the mark of a highly respected person. Even among friends, long periods of silence often preceded talk.

In the following selection, Dr. Charles Eastman, a native Sioux, evaluates and praises these virtues of Indian character. An expert commentator on this subject, Dr. Eastman spent his life in two societies, among two peoples, the Indian and the white. Until the age of fifteen he roamed the territory of the upper Missouri and lower Canada with the Sioux. Then his father, who had been captured and presumed killed by the whites many years before, returned to the tribe, a convert to white civilization. The father took his son back to the Dakota Territory where the youth was initiated into the ways of the white man. His name was changed from Ohiyesa to Charles Alexander Eastman, and he was sent to the Santee training school. He later attended Beloit College in Wisconsin, and graduated from Dartmouth College. From 1887 until 1890 Eastman studied medicine at Boston University. Upon gradu-

*ation, he returned to the Pine Ridge Agency in South Dakota
to serve his people as a physician.*

*Soon Dr. Eastman's work for the Sioux led him into the
field of administration. He left Pine Ridge for Washington,
D.C., where he represented the Sioux in land claims cases.
Often he was asked to appear before Senate and House com-
mittees on Indian Affairs. He established personal relationships with Presidents Harrison, Cleveland, McKinley, and
Roosevelt.*

*Motivated by his interest in preserving knowledge of the
Indian way of life, Dr. Eastman wrote nearly a dozen books
on Indian life and culture. Best known among them are* The
Soul of the Indian, From the Deep Woods to Civilization,
Indian Boyhood, *and* The Indian Today. The Soul of the
Indian, *from which the following selection is taken, was
published in 1911.*

As a child I understood how to give; I have forgotten this
grace since I became civilized. I lived the natural life, whereas
I now live the artificial. Any pretty pebble was valuable to
me then; every growing tree an object of reverence. Now I
worship with the white man before a painted landscape
whose value is estimated in dollars! Thus the Indian is re-
constructed as the natural rocks are ground to powder and
made into artificial blocks which may be built into the walls
of modern society.

The first American mingled with his pride a singular
humility. Spiritual arrogance was foreign in his nature and
teaching. He never claimed that the power of articulate
speech was proof of superiority over the dumb creation; on
the other hand, it is to him a perilous gift. He believes pro-
foundly in silence—the sign of a perfect equilibrium. Silence
is the absolute poise or balance of body, mind, and spirit.
The man who preserves his selfhood is ever calm and un-
shaken by the storms of existence—not a leaf, as it were,
astir on the tree; not a ripple upon the surface of the shining
pool—his, in the mind of the unlettered sage, is the ideal
attitude and conduct of life.

If you ask him: "What is silence?" he will answer: "It is the Great Mystery!" "The holy silence is His voice!" If you ask: "What are the fruits of silence?" he will say: "They are self-control, true courage of endurance, patience, dignity, and reverence. Silence is the cornerstone of character."

"Guard your tongue in youth," said the old chief, Wabashaw, "and in age you may mature a thought that will be of service to your people!"

2

"Childhood in an Indian Village"

by Wilfred Pelletier

*The nature of Indian values and their difference from west-
ern white values may be clearly shown in the lifestyle and
activities of Indian children. In the selection which follows,
Wilfred Pelletier, an Odawa Indian, reminisces about his
life as a child in an Indian village. Looking back he empha-
sizes the noncompetitive form of life he enjoyed as a young
boy, the integration of work and play within the Indian
community, and the horizontal power structure within the
village.*

*The way of life which Wilfred Pelletier experienced in
the Indian community of his youth sprang from a deep
concern for the sanctity of human life. Children were free to
learn and grow on their own, unhampered by arbitrary rules.
Community action stemmed not from an organized bu-
reaucratized structure, but from tribal consciousness.*

*By invading the Indian villages, trying to organize them,
trying to replace inherent Indian values with alien competitive and materialistic values, government agencies have totally
disrupted the natural life of Indian communities. The reac-
tion of the Indian has been to withdraw, to reject totally that
culture which wishes to assimilate him. Yet, the writer of
the following essay sees hope in the future, hope that someday*

the humanistic values of the Indian will be adopted by the larger white society.

Wilfred Pelletier was born in the village of Wikwemikong on Ontario's Manitolin Island. He is on the staff of the Institute for Indian Studies at Rochdale College, an informal learning community in Toronto.

Going back as far as I can remember as a child in an Indian community, I had no sense of knowing about the other people around me except that we were all somehow equal; the class structure in the community was horizontal. There was only one class. Nobody was interested in getting on top of anybody else.

You could see it in our games. Nobody organized them. There weren't any competitive sports. But we were involved in lots of activity (I was not like I am now; I was in pretty good shape at that time) and we were organized, but not in the sense that there were ways of finding out who had won and who had lost. We played ball like everyone else, but no one kept score. In fact, you would stay up at bat until you hit the ball. If somebody happened to walk by on the street, an old guy, we'd tease him and bug him to come over and try to hit the ball, and he would come over and he'd swing away. If they threw us out on first, we'd stay on first anyway. We ran to second, and they would throw us out there, and sometimes we'd get thrown out all the way around.

We had a number of other games we used to play. There was one where we used to try and hit each other between two lines with a ball. It didn't really make any difference if you got hit or whether you stayed in the center and tried to hit the other guy or not. But it was very, very difficult to hit these guys. I remember standing between these two lines, and all of a sudden the guys would take off, and you could be two or three feet from them, and you would have to throw the ball at them, and you just couldn't hit those guys. They were really terrific.

It was later on in life that I began to realize that what we

were really doing was *playing*. Very much like animals play.
When you observe the bear, the adults, the male and female
are always playing with the cubs. The otters do the same
thing. None of the kind of play we had was really structured
and organized. That came after the recreation directors from
the outside world came in and told us that we had a problem
in the community, that we were not organized, and they were
going to introduce some [organization].

They introduced them all right, and the tremendous competitiveness that went with them. It's not as bad on Mani-
toulin Island, where I'm from, as it is a lot of other places
where competitiveness is rolling in. I'm glad I can remember
that as a kid I was able to become involved with a community
with others and nobody was competing. Even if we did formally compete in the games we played, no one was a winner
though someone may have won. It was only the moment. If
you beat someone by pulling a bow and arrow and shooting
the arrow further, it only meant that you shot the arrow
further at that moment. That's all it lasted. It didn't mean
you were better in any way whatsoever. It just meant that at
that particular time the arrow went further; maybe it was
just the way you let the bow go. These kinds of things are
very important to me and that is why I am talking about
them and, probably, exploring while I'm talking, now. When
I get the opportunity to listen to myself the odd time, I try
to explore those kinds of things that I can remember as a
child.

One of the very important things was the relationship we
had with our families. We didn't always live at home. We
lived wherever we happened to be at that particular time
when it got dark. If you were two or three miles away from
home, then that is where you slept. People would feed you
even if they didn't know who you were. We'd spend an evening, perhaps, with an old couple, and they would tell us
stories. Most of these stories were legends, and they were told
to us mostly in the winter time. In the summer people would
generally take us out and we would do a number of things

which in some way would allow us to learn about life and what it was all about: that is, by talking about some particular person and demonstrating what that person did. At no time, in all the years I spent there, do I ever remember anyone teaching us anything.

I have been to numerous communities across Canada and I still do not find where Indians teach. All young children were allowed to grow, to develop, to learn. They didn't teach you that this was mommy, daddy, desk, ash tray, house, etc. We learned about these things by listening to the words adults spoke, what they said when they were talking, and built our own kind of relationship with the article. If you observe your children now you will see a child turn a chair over, cover it with a blanket and use it for a house. He can relate many ways to a chair. As we get older we have only one relationship and that is to stick our rear ends on that chair. It's for no other purpose, and, in fact, we tell our kids that that is what it is, and it belongs in a corner and don't move it out of there.

These things I remember very well. We were brought up to have a different relationship to a house and to all the things that surrounded us. That is, the values that adults placed on things in the community did not necessarily carry over into their child and lead him to place the same values on them. Children discovered the values of these things on their own, and developed their own particular relationship to them.

This is very closely related to the religion of the community, which centered entirely on man. One of the practiced ethics of the community was non-interference. No one interfered with us, and this way of living still exists today. If you go to an Indian home the kids don't come up and bug you while you are talking to someone else. They might come and stand by you quietly, just as an adult might. If you observe Indians someplace, they will stand quietly, and only when they are acknowledged will they speak. If they get into a group session, they will act the same way. They will sit and listen to people talk, and when they get the opportunity they will speak, but they won't cut you off or interfere. There are some who do this now, but not very many. Most of them will just wait. The whole background in the educational system was that of observing and feeling. This is how they learned.

It was a very different kind of learning situation that we were in as children. In fact, all of the things we did related to our way of life. Everything had to fit into the whole; we didn't learn things in parts. As an example: if we watched someone running an outboard motor, we would learn everything that was involved in working that motor. If someone taught someone here to do that, after he was finished he might add a safety program on top of it. This would be an additional thing. The way Indians learned it, they built in a safety program while they were learning through their observations and because their very lives depended on their doing it right.

And just as we didn't separate our learning from our way of life, we didn't separate our work from it either. The older women, for example, who used to work all day at whatever— tanning hides, etc.—didn't really think of it as work. It was a way of life. That's the real difference between the kind of society we have now where we equate these kinds of things with work and yet will go out and play sports and enjoy it, and the kind of society I'm talking about. Here, we go and work and use maybe half or a quarter of the energy we spend playing sports, but we call it work and we feel differently about it altogether. These are the kinds of differences that exist. Indian people who had a way of life and who felt it was their way of life didn't call it work. It was part of the way they provided for their families; and they "worked" very hard.

One of the reasons, of course, why they didn't call it "work" was that they didn't have any foremen. As I mentioned before, there wasn't any kind of a vertical structure in the community. In these communities, what existed was a sharing of power. In spite of what everybody says, we really didn't have chiefs, that is, people who were bosses. We had medicine men, who were wise men. The rest were leaders in particular ways. They weren't leaders as we look at them today. It was a different kind of leadership in that the person who was leader had special abilities, say in fishing or hunting. He took the leadership that day, and then discarded the leadership when he was finished with the job. He had power only for the time he wanted to do something. That power came in all forms of all the things he did in the community, so that he used power only for the things he wanted to do, and then he immediately shed it so that someone else could pick it up. It could change hands several times in the community in a day or a week or whatever.

Only in times of war and disaster was a vertical structure used. The war chief would designate various jobs to various people and use that vertical structure. This was only in times of danger. Otherwise, it was horizontal. My grandfather one time told me this, although it didn't sink in until just a few years ago, that to have power is destructive. You'll be destructive if you have power because if people don't join you, then you will destroy them. I forgot this and dug around for power and began to lose friends. I was making decisions for people even with the background I have. Now I have such a problem fighting this thing off, because people are always putting me in a position where I have power. They say I am director of the Institute of Indian Studies. This is not true. I am just at Rochdale College. [Rochdale College is a residential anti-university. Not much is happening academically, but the creative arts flourish. The College contains an Indian Institute which holds seminars and does some organizing in Canadian Indian communities.—Editor.] Where I am everyone makes up their own minds in terms of what they want to do, and they do these things, and if I can be of assistance, then I assist. I've got my own thing that I hope to do. One of the things that I'm interested in is the kind of lives that the young Indian people now at Rochdale live—what is happening to them in the city.

The city has special problems for them as it had for me.

For many of them were raised in Indian homes, where the attitude is that no child ever should be rejected. In an Indian home, if a child's face is dirty or his diaper is wet, he is picked up by anyone. The mother or father or whoever comes into the house. He is never rejected. And they don't stick children in cribs, where they can only look in one direction —up. The child generally sits or stands (often tied in), so he can relate to the world in all directions. And children are fed whenever they are hungry. They are never allowed to be in want. Whatever is wanted is given to them. If a child wants to play with something, it is always placed in his hand. No one would think of putting a rattle slightly out of reach, so he would try to grab it and be aggressive. No one would think of feeding the baby only at set times. What follows this approach in terms of attitudes and way of life is immense. The child's nature is very strongly influenced in the first four or five years. The children become very non-competitive. They have no need to compete.

The whole situation changes, however, when they go out into the world, where the attitudes and values are totally different. A world, further, in which their values are not acceptable. Where for many of us as children we were not even permitted to speak our own language. Of course, we still tried to speak our own language, but we were punished for it. Four or five years ago they were still stripping kids of their clothes up around Kenora and beating them for speaking their own language. It is probably still happening in many other institutions today. I was punished several times for speaking Indian not only on the school grounds but off the school grounds and on the street, and I lived across from the school. Almost in front of my own door my first language was forbidden me, and yet when I went into the house my parents spoke Indian.

Our language is so important to us as a people. Our language and our language structure related to our whole way of life. How beautiful that picture language is where they only tell you the beginning and the end, and you fill in everything, and they allow you to feel how you want to feel. Here we manipulate and twist things around and get you to hate a guy. The Indian doesn't do that. He'll just say that some guy got into an accident, and he won't give you any details. From there on you just explore as far as you want to. You'll say: "What happened?" and he'll tell you a little more. "Did he go through the windshield?" "Yep!" He only answers questions. All of the in-between you fill in for yourself as you see it. We are losing that feeling when we lose our language at school. We are taught English, not Indian, as our first language. And that changes our relationship with our parents. All of a sudden we begin saying to our parents "you're stupid." We have begun to equate literacy with learning, and this is the first step down. It is we who are going down and not our parents, and because of that separation we are going down lower and lower on the rung because it is we who are rejecting our parents; they are not rejecting us. The parents know that, but they are unable to do anything about it. And we take on the values, and the history of somebody else.

And part of the reason our parents say so little is that that's their way. They don't teach like white people; they let their children make their own decisions. The closest they ever got to formal teaching was to tell us stories. Let me give you an example. We had been out picking blueberries one time, and while sitting around this guy told us this story. The idea was that he wanted to get us to wash up—to wash our feet because we had been tramping through this brush all day long. He talked about a warrior who really had a beautiful body. He was very well built, and he used to grease himself and take care of his body. One day this warrior was out, and he ran into a group of other people whom he had never seen before. They started to chase him. He had no problem because he was in such good shape. He was fooling around and playing with them because he was such a good runner. He ran over hills and over rocks, teasing them. Then he ran into another group. The first group gave up the chase. But now he had to run away from this other group, and he was fooling around doing the same thing with them. All of a sudden he ran into a third group. He ran real hard and all of a sudden he fell. He tried to get up and he couldn't. He spoke to his feet and said, "What's wrong with you? I'm going to get killed if you don't get up and get going." They said, "That's alright. You can comb your hair and grease your body and look after your legs and arms but you never did anything for us. You never washed us or cleaned us or greased us or nothing." He promised to take better care of the feet if they would get up and run, and so they did.

This is one of the stories we were told, and we went up and washed our feet right away and then went to bed. Maybe this happens among other ethnic groups, I don't know, but this is the kind of learning we had. I will never forget the kinds of things we learned, because to me it all belongs to me. It isn't something that someone says is so; it's mine. I'd want to go hunting, and the guys would know I couldn't get across the stream because it was flooded, but they wouldn't say anything. They'd let me go, and I'd tell them I'd see them later where the rocks are, and they'd say O.K. knowing all this time I couldn't get through. But they wouldn't tell me that. They'd let me experience it. And I'm grateful to these people for allowing me to have this kind of exploration/learning situation. Secondly, of course, the fact is that maybe I could have gotten across where they couldn't, discovered something different, a method that was new. I think this kind of learning situation is one of the really important things that Indians have today and which could contribute to the society we have today. That is, a learning situation *for people,* instead of teaching or information giving.

All these things—the various ways Indian life differed from that of our present society—I didn't learn until after I left the reserve community later on in life. Then I could understand how very differently structured the two communities are. While it didn't have a vertical structure, our community was very highly structured. So highly structured that there wasn't anything that could happen that somebody couldn't almost immediately, in some way, solve, whatever problem arose. Without any given signals or the appearance of any communication whatsoever (there were no telephones) the most complex social action used to happen. If somebody died in that community, nobody ever said: We should dig a grave. The grave was dug, the box was made, everything was set up . . . the one who baked pies baked pies. Everyone did something in that community, and if you tried to find out who organized it, you couldn't.

It's exactly the same way today. You cannot find out who organizes these things. In 1964, Prime Minister Pearson came up to the reserve. He had a cocktail party in the hall, and at the same time there was a big buffet organized for him. This was organized by a woman from Toronto. She went up there and set the whole thing up. He had been coming there every year. This was his riding. Every year they turned out a beautiful meal for him, and he never knew who to thank because it was just all of a sudden there; it was done. The people just got together. There was no foreman or boss. There was no vertical structure, and it just happened. You should have been there in '64. It was chaotic. There were no knives, no desserts, nobody had cut up the heads of lettuce that were all over, because this woman came there and gave orders, and the people wouldn't do anything until she told them what to do. She got so busy that she couldn't tell everybody what to do, and she had four or five turkeys all over the town in different people's ovens, and that's where they sat. They had to go and tell the women to bring the turkeys down because they wouldn't do it on their own. There was someone in charge. Had there not been anyone in charge it would have gone off fine. It was a real mess. This is the difference. Here you organize, and you know those kinds of structures, and they mean something to you. You instinctively behave in certain ways to those things.

But it's more than that too. As I see it, organization comes out of a need for immediate order—say in war. When it develops this way so that people say let's organize, and they get together and create a vertical structure, and place somebody up at the top and then it becomes a power group, and from there on it filters on down until after a while you have somebody running that organization, two or three people or maybe eventually just one, and all the rest of the people get suppressed, pushed down, and held down by that very thing they formally sought. You give power to someone and suppress others.

I don't know if a different kind of structural organization can exist today. I know some people are trying to make a different one—some people in Rochdale College, and I suspect in many places where people are getting together and trying to live communally. I remember as a child a different kind of organization existing, and I have come to call it now "community consciousness." That community can exist and function and solve all its problems without any kinds of signals, like a school of fish. All of a sudden you see them move; they shift altogether. That is exactly the way most Indian communities function. And yet we have the Department of Indian Affairs coming and telling us we have no organization. The local priest or minister will come and tell us we have to be organized. The Recreation Department will come along and say there's no organization in this community. And when they come it's like shooting a goose in a flock of geese. When you hit him you disrupt the pattern. So every time somebody comes into the community they disrupt the pattern. Every time you remove a resource person from the community you disrupt the pattern. You break it up, and they have to reorganize. But in a lot of communities this is very hard to do, and some of them have been too hurt to make it. Indian resource people begin to drop out of sight and white organizers take over, making it even more difficult for Indian people to function. I know that in one community where there are 740 people (about two-thirds of them children), there are eighteen organizations. There are three churches that all have two or three organizations, and there is also a community de-

velopment officer who has a number of organizations behind
him, and they are in such conflict that the community cannot
function. It's just sitting there, with people at each other's
throats. The people who come in can't understand if a guy
is sitting under a tree and doing nothing but observing the
stars or the clouds in the daytime or the birds flying, he is
running through a recreational pattern and at the same time
he is learning. These are all parts of a whole. Most Indian
people deal with wholeness. It is much different than the way
we deal with things where we segment them and deal with
them only in parts.

It is also very difficult to know what to do now—now that
the organizers have come in. The dependency is so great and
government and outside resources have created this dependency. They have removed most of the human resource and
certainly all the economic base from most Indian communities
and there is very little left. Yet the Indian relationship to that
dependency is much different from ours in this society. Indians may receive welfare, but most of them feel it is a right.
They don't look down on people who are on welfare. Drawing
welfare doesn't change the nature of the person. In the same
way, if they walk into a room that is messy they don't say
the woman is sloppy. A lot of them don't paint their houses.
That is because they don't have the same relationship to that
house that we in this society do. Clothes don't make the man.
Relationships are built on something that is not materialistic.
The same thing applies to money. If you observe your children when they have money, they want to get rid of it right
away. How long do children stay mad at one another? A
moment. All of these behavior patterns that you observe in
children are very much related to adult Indians. Your history
books say that when the white men first came here they noted
that the Indians were very child-like. That is very true in
many ways. But if you look at it, how beautiful to be child-
like and yet be mature. Here we say that you mustn't show
feelings. I don't agree with that. If a man can cry, then he has
feelings. Indians cry all the time. We get together and sing

songs, and we cry in these songs. But this society is very machine-like, and so we begin to act like machines and then we become machines.

Because of this approach Indians don't really want to fight for their rights. They really don't want to get into the society at all. In this way they are probably different from the black people on this continent who are a much larger group, and have no choice but to fight for their rights. When they get these rights, what they are doing in essence is moving into society. When they do get in, they might make the changes they want in terms of their cultural background or how they look at things, or whatever, and these changes may give them the freedom to practice or do those things they want to do.

But the Indians have fundamentally rejected society as it now is. The Indians are expert at making all programs that the Indian Affairs Branch has ever come up with a failure by withdrawing. The Indians embrace everything that comes into a community. If you want to build a church, that's fine. We'll help you build that church, etc. Then once they see that they can't relate to that church in any way, they withdraw and the thing falls apart. If you want to build a road, they'll help you build one, with the result that some reserves have roads running all over the place, but nobody uses them. The Branch has a history of complete failure. The Indians have always rejected it. We have a society here where we must win. For everything you do you must end up fighting—fighting for your rights, good against evil, war against poverty, the fight for peace. The whole base of Western culture has an enemy concept. What would happen if you remove the enemy? How then do you defeat somebody who is on your side? I suspect that if you remove the enemy the culture might collapse. The Indian can't fight on your terms. For a start he doesn't even have the numbers, much less the inclination. So he withdraws. And he pays a certain price. He suffers poverty in many ways.

But maybe the future is with the Indian. Marshall Mc-Luhan says that the only people living in the twenty-first century are the Indians, the Eskimos, some French people and the Japanese. All the rest, because they deal with history, live in the nineteenth century because they deal with the past and not the present. The pan-Indian movement, with the Native American Church, recognizes this and there are various Indian cultures that are moving closer and closer together. It's a spontaneous thing that just happened. It's just growing and there isn't anyone who is heading it up. It's a movement. And it's made me much more hopeful.

3

FROM

Indian Boyhood

by Charles A. Eastman

The upbringing of children is a major concern for people everywhere. In every society parents wish to imbue in their children a respect for their own values and customs. They also wish to train their children so that they may become capable adults. The methods of the American Indian may serve as an example to all parents. Indian children were never beaten; they were always treated with respect and in this way learned respect. Discipline was invoked by love, not by force. Discipline was dictated by the needs of the family and the tribe, not for the sake of authority.

At an early age Indian children began preparing for their future social roles. Boys were trained in the skills of the hunter and warrior. Girls learned to cook, to make clothing, and to build shelters. Both were instructed in the legends and traditions of their people.

In the following selection Charles Eastman relates the story of his own training for the Indian life. Under the tutelage of a strict but loving uncle he learned the skills necessary to survive in the wilderness. He was instructed in the ways of the animals so that he could outwit them. He learned the ways of war so that he could defeat an enemy. Most important, he learned to be a brave man and a respectable member of his tribe.

*   *   *

It is commonly supposed that there is no systematic education of their children among the aborigines of this country. Nothing could be farther from the truth. All the customs of this primitive people were held to be divinely instituted, and those in connection with the training of children were scrupulously adhered to and transmitted from one generation to another.

The expectant parents conjointly bent all their efforts to the task of giving the new-comer the best they could gather from a long line of ancestors. A pregnant Indian woman would often choose one of the greatest characters of her family and tribe as a model for her child. This hero was daily called to mind. She would gather from tradition all of his noted deeds and daring exploits, rehearsing them to herself when alone. In order that the impression might be more distinct, she avoided company. She isolated herself as much as possible, and wandered in solitude, not thoughtlessly, but with an eye to the impression given by grand and beautiful scenery.

The Indians believed, also, that certain kinds of animals would confer peculiar gifts upon the unborn, while others would leave so strong an adverse impression that the child might become a monstrosity. A case of hare-lip was commonly attributed to the rabbit. It was said that a rabbit had charmed the mother and given to the babe its own features. Even the meat of certain animals was denied the pregnant woman, because it was supposed to influence the disposition or features of the child.

Scarcely was the embryo warrior ushered into the world, when he was met by lullabies that speak of wonderful exploits in hunting and war. Those ideas which so fully occupied his mother's mind before his birth are now put into words by all about the child, who is as yet quite unresponsive to their appeals to his honor and ambition. He is called the future defender of his people, whose lives may depend upon his courage and skill. If the child is a girl, she is at once addressed as the future mother of a noble race.

In hunting songs, the leading animals are introduced; they come to the boy to offer their bodies for the sustenance of his tribe. The animals are regarded as his friends, and spoken of almost as tribes of people, or as his cousins, grandfathers and grandmothers. The songs of wooing, adapted as lullabies, were equally imaginative, and the suitors were often animals personified, while pretty maidens were represented by the mink and the doe.

Very early, the Indian boy assumed the task of preserving and transmitting the legends of his ancestors and his race. Almost every evening a myth, or a true story of some deed done in the past, was narrated by one of the parents or grandparents, while the boy listened with parted lips and glistening eyes. On the following evening, he was usually required to repeat it. If he was not an apt scholar, he struggled long with his task; but, as a rule, the Indian boy is a good listener and has a good memory, so that the stories were tolerably well mastered. The household became his audience, by which he was alternately criticized and applauded.

This sort of teaching at once enlightens the boy's mind and stimulates his ambition. His conception of his own future career becomes a vivid and irresistible force. Whatever there is for him to learn must be learned; whatever qualifications are necessary to a truly great man he must seek at any expense of danger and hardship. Such was the feeling of the imaginative and brave young Indian. It became apparent to him in early life that he must accustom himself to rove alone and not to fear or dislike the impression of solitude.

It seems to be a popular idea that all the characteristic skill of an Indian is instinctive and hereditary. This is a mistake. All the stoicism and patience of the Indian are acquired traits, and continual practise alone makes him master of the art of wood-craft. Physical training and dieting were not neglected. I remember that I was not allowed to have beef soup or any warm drink. The soup was for the old men. General rules for the young were never to take their food very hot, nor to drink much water.

My uncle, who educated me up to the age of fifteen years,

was a strict disciplinarian and a good teacher. When I left the teepee in the morning, he would say: "Hakadah, look closely to everything you see"; and at evening, on my return, he used often to catechize me for an hour or so.

"On which side of the trees is the lighter-colored bark? On which side do they have most regular branches?"

It was his custom to let me name all the new birds that I had seen during the day. I would name them according to the color or the shape of the bill or their song or the appearance and locality of the nest—in fact, anything about the bird that impressed me as characteristic. I made many ridiculous errors, I must admit. He then usually informed me of the correct name. Occasionally I made a hit and this he would warmly commend.

He went much deeper into this science when I was a little older, that is, about the age of eight or nine years. He would say, for instance:

"How do you know that there are fish in yonder lake?"

"Because they jump out of the water for flies at mid-day."

He would smile at my prompt but superficial reply.

"What do you think of the little pebbles grouped together under the shallow water? and what made the pretty curved marks in the sandy bottom and the little sand-banks? Where do you find the fish-eating birds? Have the inlet and the outlet of a lake anything to do with the question?"

He did not expect a correct reply at once to all the voluminous questions that he put to me on these occasions, but he meant to make me observant and a good student of nature.

"Hakadah," he would say to me, "you ought to follow the example of the shunktokecha (wolf). Even when he is surprised and runs for his life, he will pause to take one more look at you before he enters his final retreat. So you must take a second look at everything you see.

"It is better to view animals unobserved. I have been a witness to their courtships and their quarrels and have learned many of their secrets in this way. I was once the unseen spectator of a thrilling battle between a pair of grizzly bears and three buffaloes—a rash act for the bears, for it was in the moon of strawberries, when the buffaloes sharpen and polish their horns for bloody contests among themselves.

"I advise you, my boy, never to approach a grizzly's den from the front, but to steal up behind and throw your blanket or a stone in front of the hole. He does not usually rush for it, but first puts his head out and listens and then comes out very indifferently and sits on his haunches on the mound in front of the hole before he makes any attack. While he is exposing himself in this fashion, aim at his heart. Always be as cool as the animal himself." Thus he armed me against the cunning of savage beasts by teaching me how to outwit them.

"In hunting," he would resume, "you will be guided by the habits of the animal you seek. Remember that a moose stays in swampy or low land or between high mountains near a spring or lake, for thirty to sixty days at a time. Most large game moves about continually, except the doe in the spring; it is then a very easy matter to find her with the fawn. Conceal yourself in a convenient place as soon as you observe any signs of the presence of either, and then call with your birchen doe-caller.

"Whichever one hears you first will soon appear in your neighborhood. But you must be very watchful, or you may be made a fawn of by a large wild-cat. They understand the characteristic call of the doe perfectly well.

"When you have any difficulty with a bear or a wild-cat— that is, if the creature shows signs of attacking you—you must make him fully understand that you have seen him and are aware of his intentions. If you are not well equipped for a pitched battle, the only way to make him retreat is to take a long sharp-pointed pole or a spear and rush toward him. No wild beast will face this unless he is cornered and already wounded. These fierce beasts are generally afraid of the common weapon of the larger animals—the horns, and if these are very long and sharp, they dare not risk an open fight.

"There is one exception to this rule—the grey wolf will attack fiercely when very hungry. But their courage depends upon their numbers; in this they are like white men. One wolf or two will never attack a man. They will stampede a herd of buffaloes in order to get at the calves; they will rush upon a herd of antelopes, for these are helpless; but they are always careful about attacking man."

Of this nature were the instructions of my uncle, who was widely known at that time as among the greatest hunters of his tribe.

All boys were expected to endure hardships without complaint. In savage warfare, a young man must, of course, be an athlete and used to undergoing all sorts of privations. He must be able to go without food and water for two or three days without displaying any weakness, or to run for a day and a night without any rest. He must be able to traverse a pathless and wild country without losing his way either in the day or night time. He cannot refuse to do any of these things if he aspires to be a warrior.

Sometimes my uncle would waken me very early in the morning and challenge me to fast with him all day. I had to accept the challenge. We blackened our faces with charcoal, so that every boy in the village would know that I was fasting that day. Then the little tempters would make my life a misery until the merciful sun hid behind the western hills.

I can scarcely recall the time when my stern teacher began to give sudden war-whoops over my head in the morning while I was sound asleep. He expected me to leap up with perfect presence of mind, always ready to grasp a weapon of some sort and to give a shrill whoop in reply. If I was sleepy or startled and hardly knew what I was about, he would ridicule me and say that I need never expect to sell my scalp dear. Often he would vary these tactics by shooting off his gun just outside of the lodge while I was yet asleep, at the same time giving blood-curdling yells. After a time I became used to this.

When Indians went upon the war-path, it was their custom to try the new warriors thoroughly before coming to an engagement. For instance, when they were near a hostile camp, they would select the novices to go after the water and make them do all sorts of things to prove their courage. In accordance with this idea, my uncle used to send me off after water when we camped after dark in a strange place. Perhaps the country was full of wild beasts, and, for aught I knew, there might be scouts from hostile bands of Indians lurking in that very neighborhood.

Yet I never objected, for that would show cowardice. I picked my way through the woods, dipped my pail in the water and hurried back, always careful to make as little noise as a cat. Being only a boy, my heart would leap at every crackling of a dry twig or distant hooting of an owl, until, at last, I reached our teepee. Then my uncle would perhaps say: "Ah, Hakadah, you are a thorough warrior," empty out the precious contents of the pail, and order me to go a second time.

Imagine how I felt! But I wished to be a brave man as much as a white boy desires to be a great lawyer or even President of the United States. Silently I would take the pail and endeavor to retrace my footsteps in the dark.

With all this, our manners and morals were not neglected. I was made to respect the adults and especially the aged. I was not allowed to join in their discussions, nor even to speak in their presence, unless requested to do so. Indian etiquette was very strict, and among the requirements was that of avoiding the direct address. A term of relationship or some title of courtesy was commonly used instead of the personal name by those who wished to show respect. We were taught generosity to the poor and reverence for the "Great Mystery." Religion was the basis of all Indian training.

I recall to the present day some of the kind warnings and reproofs that my good grandmother was wont to give me. "Be strong of heart—be patient!" she used to say. She told me of a young chief who was noted for his uncontrollable temper. While in one of his rages he attempted to kill a woman, for which he was slain by his own band and left unburied as a mark of disgrace—his body was simply covered with green grass. If I ever lost my temper, she would say:

"Hakadah, control yourself, or you will be like that young man I told you of, and lie under a *green blanket!*"

In the old days, no young man was allowed to use tobacco in any form until he had become an acknowledged warrior and had achieved a record. If a youth should seek a wife before he had reached the age of twenty-two or twenty-three, and been recognized as a brave man, he was sneered at and considered an ill-bred Indian. He must also be a skillful hunter. An Indian cannot be a good husband unless he brings home plenty of game.

These precepts were in the line of our training for the wild life.

4

FROM

We Talk, You Listen

by Vine Deloria, Jr.

*Indian and white thinking are separated by more than dif-
ferences of opinion on specific issues. Their basic approach
to both thought and life vary greatly. The white man creates
his thought and values within the framework of a stringently
individualistic society. The Indian shapes his ideas within the
context of a tribal consciousness.*

*In the selection which follows, Vine Deloria, Jr. explains
the meaning and consequences of this difference in world
view. He sees in contemporary America the beginning of a
total change in philosophical concept and values. Now, he
believes, the white society must adopt the tribal-communal
way of Indian life if it is to survive in a humanistic form.*

*Vine Deloria, Jr., a Standing Rock Sioux, was born in
Martin, a border town on the Pine Ridge Indian Reservation in South Dakota. The son of an Episcopal minister, he
is also the lineal descendant of Sioux war chiefs. A graduate
of Iowa State University and Lutheran School of Theology,
Mr. Deloria is presently completing a law degree at the University of Colorado.*

*Formerly the Executive Director of the Congress of Ameri-
can Indians, Vine Deloria, Jr. has become a well-known commentator on contemporary Indian affairs. In addition to* We

Talk, You Listen, *which appeared in 1970, he has written* Custer Died for Your Sins, *which was published in 1969.*

Every now and then I am impressed with the thinking of the non-Indian. I was in Cleveland last year and got to talking with a non-Indian about American history. He said that he was really sorry about what had happened to Indians, but that there was good reason for it. The continent had to be developed and he felt that Indians had stood in the way and thus had had to be removed. "After all," he remarked, "what did you do with the land when you had it?" I didn't understand him until later when I discovered that the Cuyahoga River running through Cleveland is inflammable. So many combustible pollutants are dumped into the river that the inhabitants have to take special precautions during the summer to avoid accidentally setting it on fire. After reviewing the argument of my non-Indian friend I decided that he was probably correct. Whites had made better use of the land. How many Indians could have thought of creating an inflammable river?

A century ago whites broke the Fort Laramie Treaty with the Sioux so they could march into the Black Hills and dig gold out of the ground. Then they took the gold out of the Black Hills, carried it to Fort Knox, Kentucky, and buried it in the ground. Throughout the Midwest, Indians were forced off their lands because whites felt that the Indians didn't put the lands to good use. Today most of this land lies idle every year while the owners collect a government check for not planting anything. Wilderness was taken because "no one" lived there and cities were built in which no one could live. . . .

These things have set me wondering if there isn't a better way to distinguish between the Indian mood, life style, and philosophy, and that of the non-Indian. It is very difficult to do. Non-Indians are descended from a peculiar group of people. The first group thought they were sailing off the edge of the world and probably would have had we not pulled them ashore. Their successors spent years traveling all over the continent in search of the Fountain of Youth, and the Seven Cities of Gold. They didn't even know how to plant an ear of corn when they arrived on these shores. So the non-Indian is pretty set in his ideas and hard to change.

There are a great many things happening today that can be related to ideas, movements, and events in Indian country —so many that it is staggering to contemplate them. American society is unconsciously going Indian. Moods, attitudes, and values are changing. People are becoming more aware of their isolation even while they continue to worship the rugged individualist who needs no one. The self-sufficient man is casting about for a community to call his own. The glittering generalities and mythologies of American society no longer satisfy the need and desire to belong.

Trying to communicate is an insurmountable task, however, since one cannot skip readily from a tribal way of life to the conceptual world of the non-tribal person. The non-tribal person thinks in a linear sequence, in which A is the foundation for B, and C always follows. The view and meaning of the total event is rarely understood by the non-tribal person, although he may receive more objective information concerning any specific element of the situation. Non-tribals can measure the distance to the moon with unerring accuracy, but the moon remains an impersonal object to them without personal relationships that would support or illuminate their innermost feelings.

Tribal society is of such a nature that one must experience it from the inside. It is holistic, and logical analysis will only return you to your starting premise none the wiser for the trip. Being inside a tribal universe is so comfortable and reasonable that it acts like a narcotic. When you are forced outside the tribal context you become alienated, irritable, and lonely. In desperation you long to return to the tribe if only to preserve your sanity. While a majority of Indian people today live in the cities, a substantial number make long weekend trips back to their reservations to spend precious hours in their own land with their people.

The best method of communicating Indian values is to find points at which issues appear to be related. Because tribal society is integrated toward a center and non-Indian society is oriented toward linear development, the process might be compared to describing a circle surrounded with tangent lines. The points at which the lines touch the circumference of the circle are the issues and ideas that can be shared by Indians and other groups. There are a great many points at which tangents occur, and they may be considered as windows through which Indians and non-Indians can glimpse each other. Once this structural device is used and understood, non-Indians, using a tribal point of view, can better understand themselves and their relationship to Indian people.

The problem is complicated by the speed of modern communications media. It floods us with news that is news because it is reported as news. Thus, if we take a linear viewpoint of the world, the sequence of spectacular events creates the impression that the world is going either up- or downhill. Events become noted more for their supportive or threatening aspects than for their reality, since they fall into line and do not themselves contain any means of interpretation. When we are unable to absorb the events reported to us by the media, we begin to force interpretations of what the world really means on the basis of what we have been taught rather than what we have experienced.

Indian people are just as subject to the deluge of information as are other people. In the last decade most reservations have come within the reach of television and computers. In many ways Indian people are just as directed by the electric nature of our universe as any other group. But the tribal viewpoint simply absorbs what is reported to it and immediately integrates it into the experience of the group. In many areas whites are regarded as a temporary aspect of tribal life and there is unshakable belief that the tribe will survive the domination of the white man and once again rule the continent. Indians soak up the world like a blotter and continue almost untouched by events. The more that happens, the better the tribe seems to function and the stronger it appears to get. Of all the groups in the modern world Indians are best able to cope with the modern situation. To the non-Indian world, it does not appear that Indians are capable of anything. The flexibility of the tribal viewpoint enables Indians to meet devastating situations and survive. But this flexibility is seen by non-Indians as incompetency, so that as the non-Indian struggles in solitude and despair he curses the Indian for not coveting the same disaster.

In 1969, non-Indians began to rediscover Indians. Everyone hailed us as their natural allies in the ancient struggle they were waging with the "bad guys." Conservatives embraced us because we didn't act uppity, refused to move into their neighborhoods, and didn't march in *their* streets. Liberals loved us because we were the most oppressed of all the peoples who had been oppressed, and besides we generally voted Democratic.

Blacks loved us because we objected to the policies of the Department of the Interior (we would probably object if we had set the damn thing up ourselves) which indicated to them that we were another group to count on for the coming revolution. I attended one conference last fall at which a number of raging militants held forth, giving their views on the upcoming revolt of the masses. In a fever pitch they described the battle of Armageddon in which the "pigs" would be vanquished and the meek would inherit the earth (or a reasonable facsimile thereof). When asked if he supported the overthrow of the establishment, an old Sioux replied, "not until we get paid for the Black Hills." Needless to say, revolutionaries have not been impressed with the Indian fervor for radical change.

Hippies proudly showed us their beads and, with a knowing smile, bid us hello in the Navajo they had learned while passing through Arizona the previous summer. We watched and wondered as they paraded by in buckskin and feathers, anxiously playing a role they could not comprehend. When the Indians of the Bay area occupied Alcatraz, the hippies descended on the island in droves, nervously scanning the horizon for a vision of man in his pristine natural state. When they found that the tribesmen had the same organizational problems as any other group might have, they left in disappointment, disillusioned with "Indianism" that had existed only in their imaginations.

For nearly a year, the various minority and power groups have tried to get Indians to relate to the social crisis that plagues the land. Churches have expended enormous sums creating "task forces" of hand-picked Indians to inform them on the national scope of Indian problems. They have been disappointed when Indians didn't immediately embrace violence as a technique for progress. Government agencies have tried to understand Indians in an urban context that no longer has validity for even the most stalwart urbanite. Conservationists have sought out Indians for their mystical knowledge of the use of land. It has been an exciting year.

There is no doubt in my mind that a major crisis exists. I believe, however, that it is deeper and more profound than racism, violence, and economic deprivation. American society is undergoing a total replacement of its philosophical concepts. Words are being emptied of old meanings and new values are coming in to fill the vacuum. Racial antagonism, inflation, ecological destruction, and power groups are all symptoms of the emergence of a new world view of man and his society. Today thought patterns are shifting from the traditional emphasis on the solitary individual to as yet unrelated definitions of man as a member of a specific group.

This is an extremely difficult transition for any society to make. Rather than face the situation head-on, people have preferred to consider social problems as manifestations of a gap between certain elements of the national community. The most blatant example of this attitude is to speak of the "generation gap." Other times it is categorized as a racial problem—the white racist power structure against the pure and peace-loving minority groups. We know that this is false. In those programs where blacks have dominated they have been as racist against Indians as they claim whites have been against them. Behind every movement is the undeniable emergence of the group as a group. Until conceptions of the nature of mass society are enlarged and accepted by the majority of people there will be little peace in this society. . . .

5

Speech of Smohalla (Nez Percé)

Much of the persecution of the American Indian arose because the Indian did not share the particular work ethic of the western Europeans who colonized America. A people's attitude toward work is a culturally determined factor. The Indians' attitude toward work was different from the white man's, and in the difference the white saw only laziness. The Indian labored to feed, clothe, and shelter himself and his tribe, but did so only when it was necessary. Work was not valued as an end in itself; more highly valued was the enjoyment of life, beauty, and wisdom.

This idea is poetically expressed in the following speech by Smohalla, a member of the Nez Percé tribe which inhabited the Great Basin area of Oregon. Smohalla's speech, made in the late nineteenth century, also reveals the intimate relationship the Indian saw between man and earth, that of a mother to a child.

A religious leader and founder of the Dreamer Religion, Smohalla strongly opposed the incursion of the white man and white civilization into the remaining Indian domains.

My young men shall never work. Men who work cannot dream, and wisdom comes in dreams.

You ask me to plow the ground. Shall I take a knife and

tear my mother's breast? Then when I die she will not take me to her bosom to rest.

You ask me to dig for stone. Shall I dig under her skin for bones? Then when I die I cannot enter her body to be born again.

You ask me to cut grass and make hay and sell it, and be rich like white men. But how dare I cut off my mother's hair?

It is a bad law, and my people cannot obey it. I want my people to stay with me here. All the dead men will come to life again. We must wait here in the house of our fathers and be ready to meet them in the body of our mother.

III

Encountering the White Man

Western history books celebrate Columbus' "discovery" of the "New World" as the beginning of the history of North America. The white invasion of America is seen as the start of a great civilization. For the native American, however, it undoubtedly would have been better if Columbus' ships had fallen over the edge of the earth.

The native Americans met the whites who landed on their shores with a combination of fear, awe, and curiosity. Friendliness soon came to dominate these emotions. Of his first encounter with the natives of Cuba, Christopher Columbus wrote:

> Of anything they have, if it be asked for, they never say no, but do rather invite the person to accept it, and show as much lovingness as though they would give their hearts. . . . And they knew no sect, nor idolatry; save that they all believe that power and goodness are in the sky, and they believed very firmly that I, with these ships and crews, came from the sky; and in such opinion, they received me at every place where I landed, after they had lost their terror. And this comes not because they are ignorant: on the contrary, they are men of very subtle wit, who navigate all those seas, and who give a marvelous good account of everything, but because they never saw men wearing clothes nor the likes of our ships. And as soon as I arrived in the Indies, in the first island I

found, I took some of them by force, to the intent that they should learn [our speech] and give me information of what there was in those parts. . . .

The Indians' friendliness and generosity was rewarded with hostility and destruction. The Spanish immediately set upon the natives, enslaving them and sending large numbers back to Spain as curiosities. There was no thought given to the idea that the natives were and should remain a sovereign people. The Spaniards felt that the aborigines should be brought under the rule of God and King—by any means necessary. This mode of conduct toward the Indians, established in the fifteenth century, was followed by the early colonists of North America and later adopted by the United States Government.

This behavior of the whites was incomprehensible to the Indian. In a speech delivered to John Smith in 1609, Powhatan eloquently articulated the feelings of the American Indian:

> Why will you take by force what you may have quietly by love? Why will you destroy us who supply you with food? What can you get by war? We can hide our provisions and run into the woods; then you will starve for wronging your friends. Why are you jealous of us? We are unarmed, and willing to give you what you ask, if you come in a friendly manner, and not with swords and guns, as if to make war upon an enemy. I am not so simple as not to know that it is much better to eat good meat, sleep comfortably, live quietly with my wives and children, laugh and be merry with the English, and trade for their copper and hatchets, than to run away from them, and to lie cold in the woods, feed on acorns, roots and such trash, and be so hunted that I can neither eat nor sleep. . . . Take away your guns and swords, the cause of all our jealousy, or you may all die in the same manner.

These words went unheeded by the whites. The quest for land and unwillingness to consider any civilization but their own worthy of survival deafened them to the sensible message of the Indians. For the next 300 years the whites continued to war against the native peoples of America, introducing disease and decadence into once flourishing tribes.

The following section contains narrative accounts of encounters between whites and Indians during the nineteenth century. It is a sad and shameful history, but it must be told. For too long white Americans have ignored the fact that their entire civilization has its origins in theft and murder. The "Indian Wars" must be seen for what they were: wars of extermination, cruel and concerted efforts toward the genocide of the Indian peoples. Non-Indian readers may learn from Chief Red Fox, a Sioux, and John Stands in Timber, a Cheyenne, the true history of the Custer battle. From Black Elk the reader will hear the horrifying story of the massacre at Wounded Knee Creek.

American society has luxuriated in a history of myth for too long a time. If this country is to accede to the greatness it proclaims, its people must study their true history, the history that has been remembered and recorded by the Indian.

1

FROM

Bury My Heart at Wounded Knee

by Dee Brown

The atrocities perpetuated by the U.S. Government upon the Sioux Indians at Wounded Knee defy human understanding. Equal in horror to the slayings of unarmed Vietnamese civilians at My Lai, the true history of Wounded Knee has lain buried for almost 100 years.

By 1890 a messianic religion had spread among the despairing Indians of America. Reduced to hunger and poverty, restricted to life on reservations, the Indians found hope and release in a revivalistic religion whose worship included the performance of the classical Sun Dance. Ignorant of Indian culture, the government saw in this increase of religious activity the threat of an Indian offensive. The revered Chief Sitting Bull was arrested, although he had not taken an active part in the new religion. Shortly after his arrest, he was assassinated on the Standing Rock Reservation.

This event greatly alarmed Chief Big Foot whose people were peacefully occupying the Cheyenne River Reservation in accordance with Red Cloud's treaty of 1868. Even more alarming was the news that the Sioux in Big Foot's encampment were to be taken into military custody. Agitated by this information, the tribe, which was already starving due to an unexplained decrease in their government food ration, decided to travel to the Pine Ridge Reservation, seeking both food and safety.

Three hundred fifty men, women, and children began the 150 mile journey through the frigid Dakota winter. On the outskirts of the Pine Ridge Reservation the tribe spotted soldiers: the Seventh Cavalry, the most hated and feared military force in the West. Big Foot hoisted a white flag and the tribe was immediately surrounded by machine guns. Commanded to march into the army camp at Wounded Knee Creek, the Indians settled for the night, hoping to continue to Pine Ridge in the morning.

The next morning the soldiers ordered the Minneconjou Sioux to relinquish all of their arms. All weapons and even hunting and building tools were taken from them. Supposedly a scuffle occurred during the search for weapons and a gun went off. Whether this was true or not, an organized fire assault rained down upon the unprotected Sioux. Infantry, cavalry, and machine gun fire tore through the wretched encampment. Within minutes 200 Indian women and children and 90 men were either killed or mortally wounded.

The following account of the slaughter at Wounded Knee was written by Dee Brown, a prominent author of histories about American Indians. Mr. Brown has written fifteen books dealing with the old West. He is currently a librarian at the University of Illinois. Bury My Heart at Wounded Knee *was published in 1970.*

Had it not been for the sustaining force of the Ghost Dance religion, the Sioux in their grief and anger over the assassination of Sitting Bull might have risen up against the guns of the soldiers. So prevalent was their belief that the white men would soon disappear and that with the next greening of the grass their dead relatives and friends would return, they made no retaliations. By the hundreds, however, the leaderless Hunkpapas fled from Standing Rock, seeking refuge in one of the Ghost Dance camps or with the last of the great chiefs, Red Cloud, at Pine Ridge. In the Moon When the Deer Shed

Their Horns (December 17) about a hundred of these fleeing Hunkpapas reached Big Foot's Minneconjou camp near Cherry Creek. That same day the War Department issued orders for the arrest and imprisonment of Big Foot. He was on the list of "fomenters of disturbances."

As soon as Big Foot learned that Sitting Bull had been killed, he started his people toward Pine Ridge, hoping that Red Cloud could protect them from the soldiers. En route, he fell ill of pneumonia, and when hemorrhaging began, he had to travel in a wagon. On December 28, as they neared Porcupine Creek, the Minneconjous sighted four troops of cavalry approaching. Big Foot immediately ordered a white flag run up over his wagon. About two o'clock in the afternoon he raised up from his blankets to greet Major Samuel Whitside, Seventh U.S. Cavalry. Big Foot's blankets were stained with blood from his lungs, and as he talked in a hoarse whisper with Whitside, red drops fell from his nose and froze in the bitter cold.

Whitside told Big Foot that he had orders to take him to a cavalry camp on Wounded Knee Creek. The Minneconjou chief replied that he was going in that direction; he was taking his people to Pine Ridge for safety.

Turning to his half-breed scout, John Shangreau, Major Whitside ordered him to begin disarming Big Foot's band. "Look here, Major," Shangreau replied, "if you do that, there is liable to be a fight here; and if there is, you will kill all those women and children and the men will get away from you."

Whitside insisted that his orders were to capture Big Foot's Indians and disarm and dismount them.

"We better take them to camp and then take their horses from them and their guns," Shangreau declared.

"All right," Whitside agreed. "You tell Big Foot to move down to camp at Wounded Knee." [1]

The major glanced at the ailing chief, and then gave an order for his Army ambulance to be brought forward. The

1. Utley, Robert M. *The Last Days of the Sioux Nation.* (New Haven: Yale University Press, 1963), p. 195.

ambulance would be warmer and would give Big Foot an easier ride than the jolting springless wagon. After the chief was transferred to the ambulance, Whitside formed a column for the march to Wounded Knee Creek. Two troops of cavalry took the lead, the ambulance and wagons following, the Indians herded into a compact group behind them, with the other two cavalry troops and a battery of two Hotchkiss guns bringing up the rear.

Twilight was falling when the column crawled over the last rise in the land and began descending the slope toward Chankpe Opi Wakpala, the creek called Wounded Knee. The wintry dusk and the tiny crystals of ice dancing in the dying light added a supernatural quality to the somber landscape. Somewhere along this frozen stream the heart of Crazy Horse lay in a secret place, and the Ghost Dancers believed that his disembodied spirit was waiting impatiently for the new earth that would surely come with the first green grass of spring.

At the cavalry tent camp on Wounded Knee Creek, the Indians were halted and carefully counted. There were 120 men and 230 women and children. Because of the gathering darkness, Major Whitside decided to wait until morning before disarming his prisoners. He assigned them to a camping area immediately to the south of the military camp, issued them rations, and as there was a shortage of tepee covers, he furnished them with several tents. Whitside ordered a stove placed in Big Foot's tent and sent a regimental surgeon to administer to the sick chief. To make certain that none of his prisoners escaped, the major stationed two troops of cavalry as sentinels around the Sioux tepees, and then posted his Hotchkiss guns on top of a rise overlooking the camp. The barrels of these rifled guns, which could hurl explosive charges for more than two miles, were positioned to rake the length of the Indian lodges.

Later in the darkness of that December night the remainder of the Seventh Regiment marched in from the east and quietly bivouacked north of Major Whitside's troops. Colonel James W. Forsyth, commanding Custer's former regiment, now took charge of operations. He informed Whitside that he had received orders to take Big Foot's band to the Union Pacific Railroad for shipment to a military prison in Omaha.

After placing two more Hotchkiss guns on the slope beside the others, Forsyth and his officers settled down for the evening with a keg of whiskey to celebrate the capture of Big Foot.

The chief lay in his tent, too ill to sleep, barely able to breathe. Even with their protective Ghost Shirts and their belief in the prophecies of the new Messiah, his people were fearful of the pony soldiers camped all around them. Fourteen years before, on the Little Bighorn, some of these warriors had helped defeat some of these soldier chiefs—Moylan, Varnum, Wallace, Godfrey, Edgerly—and the Indians wondered if revenge could still be in their hearts.

"The following morning there was a bugle call," said Wasumaza, one of Big Foot's warriors who years afterward was to change his name to Dewey Beard. "Then I saw the soldiers mounting their horses and surrounding us. It was announced that all men should come to the center for a talk and that after the talk they were to move on to Pine Ridge agency. Big Foot was brought out of his tepee and sat in front of his tent and the older men were gathered around him and sitting right near him in the center."

After issuing hardtack for breakfast rations, Colonel Forsyth informed the Indians that they were now to be disarmed. "They called for guns and arms," White Lance said, "so all of us gave the guns and they were stacked up in the center." The soldier chiefs were not satisfied with the number of weapons surrendered, and so they sent details of troopers to search the tepees. "They would go right into the tents and come out with bundles and tear them open," Dog Chief said. "They brought our axes, knives, and tent stakes and piled them near the guns." [2]

Still not satisfied, the soldier chiefs ordered the warriors

2. McGregor, James H. *The Wounded Knee Massacre from the Viewpoint of the Survivors.* (Baltimore: Wirth Bros., 1940), pp. 105, 118, 134.

to remove their blankets and submit to searches for weapons. The Indians' faces showed their anger, but only the medicine man, Yellow Bird, made any overt protest. He danced a few Ghost Dance steps, and chanted one of the holy songs, assuring the warriors that the soldiers' bullets could not penetrate their sacred garments. "The prairies is large and the bullets will not go toward you." [3]

The troopers found only two rifles, one of them a new Winchester belonging to a young Minneconjou named Black Coyote. Black Coyote raised the Winchester over his head, shouting that he paid much money for the rifle and that it belonged to him. Some years afterward Dewey Beard recalled that Black Coyote was deaf. "If they had left him alone he was going to put his gun down where he should. They grabbed him and spinned him in the east direction. He was still unconcerned, even then. He hadn't his gun pointed at anyone. His intention was to put that gun down. They came on and grabbed the gun that he was going to put down. Right after they spun him around there was the report of a gun, was quite loud. I couldn't say that anybody was shot, but following that was a crash."

"It sounded much like the sound of tearing canvas, that was the crash," Rough Feather said. Afraid-of-the-Enemy described it as a "lightening crash." [4]

Turning Hawk said that Black Coyote "was a crazy man, a young man of very bad influence and in fact a nobody." He said that Black Coyote fired his gun and that "immediately the soldiers returned fire and indiscriminate killing followed." [5]

In the first seconds of the violence, the firing of carbines was deafening, filling the air with powder smoke. Among the dying who lay sprawled on the frozen ground was Big Foot. Then there was a brief lull in the rattle of arms, with small groups of Indians and soldiers grappling at close quarters, using knives, clubs, and pistols. As few of the Indians had

3. Utley, *Last Days of Sioux Nation*, p. 210.
4. McGregor, *Wounded Knee Massacre*, pp. 106, 109, 126.
5. U.S. Bureau of Ethnology. 14th Annual Report, 1892–93, pt. 2, p. 885.

arms, they soon had to flee, and then the big Hotchkiss guns on the hill opened up on them, firing almost a shell a second, raking the Indian camp, shredding the tepees with flying shrapnel, killing men, women, and children.

"We tried to run," Louise Weasel Bear said, "but they shot us like we were a buffalo. I know there are some good white people, but the soldiers must be mean to shoot children and women. Indian soldiers would not do that to white children."

"I was running away from the place and followed those who were running away," said Hakiktawin, another of the young women. "My grandfather and grandmother and brother were killed as we crossed the ravine, and then I was shot on the right hip clear through and on my right wrist where I did not go any further as I was not able to walk, and after the soldier picked me up where a little girl came to me and crawled into the blanket." [6]

When the madness ended, Big Foot and more than half of his people were dead or seriously wounded; 153 were known dead, but many of the wounded crawled away to die afterward. One estimate placed the final total of dead at very nearly three hundred of the original 350 men, women, and children. The soldiers lost twenty-five dead and thirty-nine wounded, most of them struck by their own bullets or shrapnel.

After the wounded cavalrymen were started for the agency at Pine Ridge, a detail of soldiers went over the Wounded Knee battlefield, gathering up Indians who were still alive and loading them into wagons. As it was apparent by the end of the day that a blizzard was approaching, the dead Indians were left lying where they had fallen. (After the blizzard, when a burial party returned to Wounded Knee, they found the bodies, including Big Foot's, frozen into grotesque shapes.)

The wagonloads of wounded Sioux four men and forty-seven women and children) reached Pine Ridge after dark.

6. McGregor, *Wounded Knee Massacre*, pp. 111, 140.

Because all available barracks were filled with soldiers, they were left lying on the open wagons in the bitter cold while an inept Army officer searched for shelter. Finally the Episcopal mission was opened, the benches taken out, and hay scattered over the rough flooring.

It was the fourth day after Christmas in the Year of Our Lord 1890. When the first torn and bleeding bodies were carried into the candlelit church, those who were conscious could see Christmas greenery hanging from the open rafters. Across the chancel front above the pulpit was strung a crudely lettered banner: PEACE ON EARTH, GOOD WILL TO MEN.

2

FROM

Zuni Texts

by Ruth Bunzel

*War, however glorious, has its tragic side: death. The selec-
tion which follows is a narrative of the mourning ritual
practiced by a young Zuni woman whose husband was killed
by the whites. The anonymous Zuni informant recited her
narrative in her native language. The story was then tran-
scribed and translated by anthropologist Ruth Bunzel.*

*In the narrative the woman's personal feelings of sorrow
are accompanied by the recitation of a fixed form of prayer.
Of Zuni prayer Miss Bunzel writes:*

> *Prayer in Zuni is not a spontaneous outpouring of the heart.
> It is rather the repetition of a fixed formula. Only in such
> prayers as those accompanying individual offerings of corn
> meal and food is a certain amount of individual variation
> possible, and even here variation is restricted to the matter
> of abridgment or inclusiveness. The general form of the
> prayer, the phraseology and the nature of the request, con-
> form strictly to types for other prayers.*

. . . They came. They brought the ones who had been killed
by the white people. My aunts were with me. My mother,
father, my aunts, held me and went with me. I came there;

Ruth Bunzel, *Introduction to Zuni Ceremonialism*. 47th Annual Report
of the Bureau of American Ethnology (Washington, 1930).

I was pregnant. They would not let me see him, my husband. Only my mother saw him. She told me. It was not good. . . . So they buried them in the graveyard, just before sunset.

. . . My grandfather took care of me. "It is very dangerous; you must fast. You must drink medicine. You must vomit. It is very dangerous. No one may touch you. It is very dangerous, you must fast. No one must touch you. You must stay alone. You must sit alone in the corner. Only your little boy may hold you. No one must touch you." Grandfather gathered medicine for me. This he soaked. He mixed it in a fine bowl. He brewed medicine. "This you will drink. You will vomit," he said to me. I was very wretched. This was very dangerous. When it was still early, when the sun had not yet risen, my grandfather took me far away. We scattered prayermeal. When we had gone far I passed it four times over my head and scattered it. One should not speak. Again with this, I sprinkled prayermeal with a prayer:

> My fathers,
> Our Sun Father.
> Our mother, Dawn,
> Coming out standing to your sacred place,
> Somewhere we shall pass you on your road.
> This from which we form our flesh,
> The white corn,
> Prayermeal,
> Shell,
> Corn pollen,
> I offer to you.
> To the Sun who is our father,
> To you I offer it.
> To you, I offer prayermeal.
> To you, I offer corn pollen.
> According to the words of my prayer,
> So may it be.
> May there be no deviation.
> Sincerely from my heart I send forth my prayers.
> To you, prayermeal, shell, I offer.

Corn pollen I offer.
According to the words of my prayer,
So may it be.

I would sprinkle prayermeal. I would inhale from the prayermeal. I would sprinkle the right kind of prayermeal....

All alone I sat. I did not eat meat, nor salt, nor grease. I fasted from meat. It was very dangerous. Much my aunt, my grandfather exhorted me. When I was young, they said to me, "Fortunate you are to be alive. Sometimes you will be happy because of something. Sometimes you will be sorrowful. You will cry. This kind of person you shall be. You are fortunate to be alive." . . . And just so I have lived. . . . If one's husband dies one will not sleep. She will lie down as if she sleeps, and when sleep overcomes her she will sleep. But after a little while she will wake, and will not sleep. She will cry, she will be lonely. She will take thought of what to do and where to go. When a child or a relative dies, one cries for them properly. Husband and wife talk together to relieve their thoughts. Then they will forget their trouble. But when one's husband dies there is no happiness. . . .

It was very dangerous. It was the same as when an enemy dies, it was very dangerous. Four mornings I vomited. And so many days I sprinkled prayermeal far off, four times. And so many days I fasted. I was still a young woman. . . .

For one year I would cry. I was thoughtful for my old husband. Then father spoke to me. Then I was happy. I did not worry. My uncle desired it for me. "It is all right, niece. Do not cry. It cannot be helped. It is ever thus. Do not think of where you have come from, but rather look forward to where you are to go. . . ."

3

"Address on the Present Condition and Prospects of the Aboriginal Inhabitants of North America"

by Maris Bryant Pierce

In its dealings with the Seneca Indians of New York State, the United States Government, in conjunction with private land companies, used every ploy, deceit, and trick possible to obtain native Indian land. In 1810 the Ogden Land Company obtained rights to purchase 198,000 acres of Seneca land for fifty cents an acre. As the company could not gain any profits on this preemptive purchase until the Indians could be induced to sell their lands, the Ogden Company began to exert pressure on the Seneca Nation to emigrate westward.

In 1826 the Senecas sold land amounting to 123,000 acres for $48,216. The land company continued its efforts to gain more Indian holdings. In 1838 a U.S. Government commissioner negotiated a treaty which stipulated that the Senecas sell all of their New York lands and emigrate to the Indian Territory beyond the Mississippi.

The legality of this treaty was contested by its Indian opponents who claimed that ratification was obtained by bribing certain chiefs. As so many allegations of fraud surrounded this treaty, the U.S. Senate did not ratify it. An amended treaty was drawn up. However, as much deception surrounded this treaty as the first. Six thousand dollars in bribes were paid to obtain the signatures of one or two tribes. Although a majority of the chiefs assembled in the Seneca council were supposed to approve the treaty, only sixteen of eighty-one did so.

During this time it was the avowed policy of the federal government to move all the Indians of the eastern seaboard beyond the Mississippi, and the government appropriated $400,000 to carry out the Seneca treaty of 1838. When the Seneca Nation appealed to the federal authorities in regard to the scheme to take away their lands, they were told that it was the settled policy of the government to remove them.

The U.S. Senate ratified the treaty on April 4, 1840. The Senecas, however, refused to adhere to the terms of this treaty. In 1842 a new agreement was reached between the Seneca Nation and the Ogden Land Company with the U.S. Government acting as arbiter. The natives were allowed to keep two of their reservations. The remaining two reservations were given to the Ogden Land Company in return for payments for both land and improvements.

It is this situation which Maris Bryant Pierce, a member of the Seneca Nation, discusses in the following selection, written in 1839. An educated man, Pierce pleads the cause of his people. He argues against the exploitation of his people by money-hungry land speculators. He argues against the removal of his people to the western wilderness where they would become prey both to hostile tribes and the hostile white border population. Finally, he argues for the preservation of his people's eastern home where they enjoy "civilization and christianity."

. . . In the first place the white man wants our land; in the next place it is said that the offer for it is liberal; in the next place that we shall be better off to remove from the vicinity of the whites and settle in the neighborhood of our fellow red men, where the woods flock with game, and the streams abound with fishes. These are the reasons offered and urged in favour of our removal.

Let us consider each of these reasons a little in detail. The fact that the whites want our land imposes no obligation on us to sell it, nor does it hold forth an inducement to do so, unless it leads them to offer a price equal in value to us. We neither know nor feel any debt of gratitude which we owe to them, in consequence of their "loving kindness or tender mercies" towards us, that should cause us to make a sacrifice of our property or our interest, to their wonted avarice and which like the mother of the horse leach, cries give, give, and is never sated.

And is the offer liberal? Of that who but ourselves are to be the final judges? If we do not deem one or two dollars an acre liberal for the land, which will, to the white man's pocket bring fifteen to fifty, I don't know that we can be held heinously criminal for our opinion. It is well known, that those who are anxious to purchase our Reservations, calculate safely on fifteen dollars the acre for the poorest, and by gradation up to fifty and more, for the other qualities. By what mode of calculation or rules of judgment, is one or two dollars a liberal offer to us, when many times that sum would be only fair to the avarice of the land speculator? Since in us is vested a perfect title to the land, I know not why we may not, when we wish, dispose of it at such prices as we may see fit to agree upon.

"But the land company have the right of purchase," it is said—granted; but they have not the right, nor we trust in God, the power, to force us to accept of their offers. And when that company finds that a whistle or a rattle, or one dollar or two, per acre, will not induce us to part with our lands, is it not in the nature of things, that they should offer better and more attractive terms? If they could not make forty-nine dollars on an acre of land, I know no reason why they would fail of trying to make forty-five, or thirty, or ten. So I see no obstacle to our selling when and at such reasonable prices as we may wish, in the *fact* that the land company have the right of purchase; nor do I see any thing extortionate in us, in an unwillingness to part with our soil, on the terms offered—nor even in *the desire,* if our lands are sold, of putting into our *own* pockets a due portion of their value.

But the point of chief importance is, shall we be better off? If our object was to return to the manners and pursuits of life which characterized our ancestors, and we could be put in a *safe, unmolested* and *durable* possession of a wilderness of game, whose streams abound in fish, we might be better off; but though that were our object, I deny that we could possess *such a territory* this side of the shores of the Pacific, with *safety, free of molestation* and in *perpetuity*.

"Westward the Star of Empire takes it away," and whenever that empire is held by the white man, nothing is safe or unmolested or enduring against his avidity for gain. Population is with rapid strides going beyond the Mississippi, and even casting its eye with longing gaze for the woody peaks of the Rocky Mountains—nay even for the surf-beaten shore of the Western Ocean. And in process of time, will not our territory there, be as subject to the wants of the whites, as that which we now occupy is? Shall we not then be as strongly solicited, and by the same arguments, to remove still farther west? But there is one condition of a removal which must certainly render it hazardous in the extreme to us. The proximity of our then situation to that of other and more warlike tribes, will expose us to constant harassing by them; and not only this, but the character of those worse than Indians, those *white borderers,* who infest, yes *infest,* the western border of the white population, will annoy us more fatally than even the Indians themselves. Surrounded thus by the natives of the soil, and hunted by such a class of whites, who neither "fear God nor regard man," how shall we be better off there than where we now are?

Having said thus much as to our condition after a removal, under the supposition that we wish to return to and continue in the habits of life which prevailed when the country was first taken possession of by the Europeans, I proceed now to say, that we do not wish so to do, and to repeat, that so far from it, we desire to renounce those habits of mind and body, and adopt in their stead, those habits and feelings—those modes of living, and acting and thinking, which result from the cultivation and enlightening of the moral and intellectual faculties of man. And on this point, I need not insult your common sense by endeavoring to show that it is *stupid folly* to suppose that a removal from our present location to the western wilds would improve our condition: What! leave a fertile and somewhat improved soil—a home in the midst of civilization and christianity, where the very breezes are redolent of improvement and exaltation—where by enduction as it were, we must be pervaded by the spirit of enterprise—where books and preaching, and conversation, and business, and conduct, whose influence we need, are all around us, so that we have but to stretch forth our hands, and open our ears, and turn our eyes to experience in full, their improving and enlightening effects; leave these! and for what? and echo answers *for what?* but methinks I hear the echo followed by the anxious guileful whisper of some government land company agent—for one or two dollars the acre and a western wilderness beyond the white man's reach, where an Eden lies in all its freshness of beauty for you to possess and enjoy. But ours, I reply, is sufficiently an Eden now, if but the emissaries of the arch fiend, not so much in the form of a serpent as of man, can be kept from its borders.

But I will relieve your patience by closing my remarks; it were perhaps needless, perhaps useless, for me to appear before you with these remarks feebly and hastily prepared as they were: but as I intimated on the outset, the crisis which has now arrived in the affairs of our people furnish the apology and reason for my so doing. And now I ask, what feature of our condition is there which should induce us to leave our present location and seek another in the western wilds? Does justice, does humanity, does religion in their relations to us demand it? Does the interest and well being of the whites require it? The plainest dictates of common sense and common honesty, answer *No!* I ask then in behalf of the New York Indians and myself, that our white brethren will not urge us to do that which justice, humanity, religion not only do not require but condemn. I ask then to let us live on, where our fathers have lived—let us enjoy the advantages which our location affords us: that thus we, who have been converted heathen, may be made meet for that inheritance which the *Father* hath promised to give to his *Son,* our Saviour: so that the deserts and waste places may be made to blossom like the rose, and the inhabitants thereof utter forth the high praises of our God.

4

FROM

Indian Boyhood

by Charles A. Eastman

To the American Indians who had not yet seen whites, stories about this new race were both fantastic and terrifying. The possession of mechanical devices such as the steamboat and the steam locomotive gave to the white man the aura of the supernatural.

Though the mastery of these technological powers awed the Indians, they were unimpressed with the social life of the whites. The importance which the white man placed on material possessions was incomprehensible to the Indian. Similarly, the idea of paying taxes and fighting in a conscriptive army amazed them.

These are the impressions which the young Sioux Ohiyesa (later known as Charles Eastman) had of the white man. They have been recorded in his autobiography, Indian Boyhood, *which was published in 1902.*

. . . I had heard marvelous things of this people. In some things we despised them; in others we regarded them as *wakan* (mysterious), a race whose power bordered upon the supernatural. I learned that they had made a "fire-boat." I could not understand how they could unite two elements which cannot exist together. I thought the water would put out the fire, and the fire would consume the boat if it had the shadow of a chance. This was to me a preposterous thing! But when I was told that the Big Knives had created a "fire-boat-walks-on-mountains" (a locomotive) it was too much to believe.

"Why," declared my informant, "those who saw this monster move said that it flew from mountain to mountain when it seemed to be excited. They said also that they believed it carried a thunder-bird, for they frequently heard his usual war-whoop as the creature sped along!"

Several warriors had observed from a distance one of the first trains on the Northern Pacific, and had gained an exaggerated impression of the wonders of the pale-face. They had seen it go over a bridge that spanned a deep ravine and it seemed to them that it jumped from one bank to the other. I confess that the story almost quenched my ardor and bravery.

Two or three young men were talking together about this fearful invention.

"However," said one, "I understand that this fire-boat-walks-on-mountains cannot move except on the track made for it."

Although a boy is not expected to join in the conversation of his elders, I ventured to ask: "Then it cannot chase us into any rough country?"

"No, it cannot do that," was the reply, which I heard with a great deal of relief.

I had seen guns and various other things brought to us by the French Canadians, so that I had already some notion of the supernatural gifts of the white man; but I had never before heard such tales as I listened to that morning. It was said that they had bridged the Missouri and Mississippi rivers, and that they made immense houses of stone and brick, piled on top of one another until they were as high as high hills. My brain was puzzled with these things for many a day. Finally I asked my uncle why the Great Mystery gave such power to the *Washichu* (the rich)—sometimes we called them by this name—and not to us Dakotas.

"For the same reason," he answered, "that he gave to Duta

the skill to make fine bows and arrows, and to Wachesne no skill to make anything."

"And why do the Big Knives increase so much more in number than the Dakotas?" I continued.

"It has been said, and I think it must be true, that they have larger families than we do. I went into the house of an *Eashicha* (a German), and I counted no less than nine children. The eldest of them could not have been over fifteen. When my grandfather first visited them, down at the mouth of the Mississippi, they were comparatively few; later my father visited their Great Father at Washington, and they had already spread over the whole country."

"Certainly they are a heartless nation. They have made some of their people servants—yes, slaves! We have never believed in keeping slaves, but it seems that these *Washichu* do! It is our belief that they painted their servants black a long time ago, to tell them from the rest, and now the slaves have children born to them of the same color!

"The greatest object of their lives seems to be to acquire possessions—to be rich. They desire to possess the whole world. For thirty years they were trying to entice us to sell them our land. Finally the outbreak gave them all, and we had already spread over the whole country."

"They are a wonderful people. They have divided the day into hours, like the moons of the year. In fact, they measure everything. Not one of them would let so much as a turnip go from his field unless he received full value for it. I understand that their great men make a feast and invite many, but when the feast is over the guests are required to pay for what they have eaten before leaving the house. I myself saw at White Cliff (the name given to St. Paul, Minnesota) a man who kept a brass drum and a bell to call people to his table; but when he got them in he would make them pay for the food!

"I am also informed," said my uncle, "but this I hardly believe, that their Great Chief (President) compels every man to pay him for the land he lives upon and all his personal goods—even for his own existence—every year! (This was his idea of taxation.) I am sure we could not live under such a law. . . .

"In war they have leaders and war-chiefs of different grades. The common warriors are driven forward like a herd of antelopes to face the foe. It is on account of this manner of fighting—from compulsion and not from personal bravery —that we count no *coup* on them. A lone warrior can do much harm to a large army of them in a bad country."

It was this talk with my uncle that gave me my first clear idea of the white man. . . .

5

FROM

The Memoirs of Chief Red Fox

By Chief William Red Fox

Popular American history texts present the Indian Wars as the unfortunate but necessary result of the God-given mandate for white domination of the North American continent. Viewed from the other side, however, this bloody conflict was the last desperate fight of a people to defend their homeland against hostile invaders.

After the Civil War the settlement of western lands by whites greatly increased. The lands of the Plains Indians became a barrier to cross-country communication. White civilization demanded roads and railroads, and the construction of the Union Pacific was begun. Soon white builders, accompanied by army troops, entered the South Dakota lands of the Sioux. This invasion was met by the Sioux both with resistance and a willingness to negotiate.

The following selection by Chief Red Fox narrates the history of Chief Red Cloud's efforts to preserve the land and way of life of the Sioux. A strong leader and able politician, Red Cloud negotiated a treaty of peace with the U.S. Government in 1868. This treaty assured the Sioux of possession of their land forever. For the white man forever lasted only a short while, until gold was found in the sacred Black Hills of the Sioux.

*Chief William Red Fox, a Sioux, was born on June 11,
1870, on the Pine Ridge Reservation. As a young boy he
lived a relatively free life while the warriors of his tribe
battled the U.S. army for possession of their lands. At the age
of six Red Fox was sent 200 miles from home to a government boarding school. Two years later he was removed to
the Carlisle Indian School in Pennsylvania. During his summers as a teenager, Red Fox worked as a seaman, beginning
a life of world-wide travel.*

*In 1893, at the age of 23, Red Fox joined Buffalo Bill's
Wild West Show. As a star attraction, he toured the United
States. During the Spanish-American War Red Fox served
with the U.S. navy in the Pacific. After the close of the War
he rejoined Buffalo Bill and travelled across Europe where
he met Edward the Seventh of England and the Kaiser of
Germany. Returning to America, Red Fox acted in western
films until 1930. At that time he began, at the age of 60, a
new career, lecturing on Indian life.*

*Chief Red Fox's autobiography, from which the following
is taken, was published in 1971, the year of his 101st birthday.
The* Memoirs *comprise a final form of journals and note-
books in which Red Fox has recorded not only the events of
his own life, but a history of his tribe before he was born.*

I now have to turn back to trails that were made and events
that occurred before I was born when the Sioux still hunted
and fished unmolested in their ancient homeland on the
Western plains and mountains. From my grandparents I
learned the folklore, rituals, and customs of my ancestors,
but here I am concerned with the sinister shadow that spread
over the land in 1865 when the government decided to build
a road from Fort Laramie deep into the Indian Territory.

When news of this reached Red Cloud, chief of the Oglalas, the largest tribe of the Sioux Nation, he protested to
Washington that building the road would scatter the buffalo
upon which the Indian depended for food and clothing. He
reminded the officials that the land belonged to the Indians,

but neither his pleas nor his protests could move ambitious men who were demanding that the territory be opened for exploitation.

Red Cloud had always been a peaceful man willing to reason together with his White brothers, counseling negotiations in times of trouble. He was not in the hereditary line that would have made him a chief, but he rose to power through the strength of his personality and his service to the tribe. His attitude began to harden when his father died from vile liquor obtained from the Whites a few years before; and now the action of the government transformed him into a bitter, warlike figure. Almost overnight he became the most influential leader of the tribes and sub-tribes that comprised the Sioux Nation. The mass of Indians numbering around 35,000 looked upon him as a commander who could lead them in war, and prevent the White man from invading their sacred lands.

When, as the Indians had expected, a detachment of troops and road-builders moved into the wilderness and established a camp, Red Cloud's spies were watching, and a company of warriors were waiting to attack. Red Cloud held them in check until a detail of workmen carrying axes and saws left the camp. When they started cutting the timber, the Indians surrounded them, and they surrendered without resistance. They were held prisoners for two weeks until Red Cloud was informed that a commission was on the way from Washington to see him. He released the prisoners, but refused to meet with the commissioners, for he felt that they did not have the authority for a council. The commission returned to Washington and reported that the Indians were in a warlike mood.

The government acted quickly and called a council at Fort Laramie. Red Cloud and other chiefs of the Sioux attended. While in session, Colonel Harry Carrington rode in with a detachment of soldiers and announced that he had orders from the government to build a string of forts all the way to the Black Hills. When the announcement was made, Red Cloud was addressing the council. He was stunned into momentary silence, then he turned to Carrington in anger. His words are not recorded, but the colonel assured him that the forts would be built—by force if necessary.

Red Cloud picked up his rifle and stalked from the room followed by the other chiefs. This was the signal for war. Red Cloud sent a call to all the Sioux tribes and appealed for help from Cheyennes who occupied the adjoining lands, and soon he had an army of 4,000 warriors assembled.

In the meantime Carrington had settled down in a camp on Piney Creek and started to build the first fort. Red Cloud's troops were deployed in the nearby hills waiting for the signal to attack. The chief waited until the timbermen, protected by troops, began cutting trees a few miles from their camp. Then he gave the signal and a band of his warriors attacked and killed the entire detachment of 81 men.

Other assaults were made against men and troops who strayed away from the protection of their camp, and Carrington was restrained from building a single fort. He informed his superiors that the task was proving to be impossible because of the opposition of the Indians.

During the months this conflict was going on not a single wagon train was permitted to enter the Sioux Territory. The warriors remained at their posts expecting the arrival of government troops in force, but they did not come. Instead, the government sent a commission to come to terms with Red Cloud. He and other chiefs of the Sioux and Cheyennes met them at Fort Laramie early in January, 1868.

At that meeting, discussions included a proposal to buy the land of the Sioux, but Red Cloud refused arbitrarily, and told the commissioners that the Indians would fight for their ancient hunting grounds and sacred lands until the last one was killed if necessary. Convinced that the Indians would follow Red Cloud into a major war, and that no persuasion or offer of money could change his decision, they agreed to redefine the Sioux Territory and give them a treaty that would assure it to them "as long as the sun shines and the grass grows."

The treaty further stipulated that the country of the North Platte, through the Black Hills to the summits of the Big Horn Mountains, be considered to be unceded Indian Territory and that no White person would be permitted to settle upon or occupy any portion of it without the consent of the Indians. The government also agreed to abandon its construction projects and withdraw all troops in the area.

The treaty was satisfactory to Red Cloud, but he refused to sign it until the garrison at Piney Creek left. He was waiting there with his warriors when the last of the troops departed, then set fire to the buildings that had been erected there. Before they passed from view beyond the hills, the smoke was spiraling toward the sky.

Red Cloud had promised to disband his warriors as soon as the government withdrew its troops and completely discarded the road and forts projects in the territory. He kept his word and never again engaged in war, but came to realize that the Indians were doomed as a people. They could not fight a successful war against the combined forces of the government and the hordes of White settlers determined to possess the land.

The treaty had been signed at Fort Laramie on November 6, 1868, and after sending his warriors back to their families and homes Red Cloud stepped down from leadership, and his name does not appear in the chronicles of conflict that followed, even in the war of 1876 or the Messiah Outbreak in 1890. He spent his last years in a house given to him by the government, on the Pine Ridge Reservation, and there he died in 1909 in his eighty-seventh year.

For a few years after the treaty was signed, the government established an agency in the Sioux Territory and peace reigned, but it was an armed peace with frequent killings as White traders, adventurers, and speculators went there hoping to gain wealth through their dealings with the Indians. The government sent small detachments of troops to the territory in order to expel the invaders and honor its treaty obligations; but the troops were too few, and the adventurers too many. It was like trying to put out a prairie fire with sprinkling cans.

Soon thereafter General George A. Custer and the Seventh Cavalry arrived in the Black Hills, reportedly to make a military survey, but in reality to investigate conditions between the Whites and the Indians. One day he discovered flecks of gold on the shoes of his horse, which confirmed persisting reports and rumors that rich deposits of this metal underlay the Black Hills.

General Custer reported his findings to Washington and geological and mining experts were sent there to make a survey. When they came out of the hills the fate of the Sioux was assured. The surveyors had indisputable evidence that gold existed in abundance there.

The news, which was flashed over the "talking wires" and printed in newspaper headlines, was discussed in financial circles, and in saloons and dance halls where miners, adventurers, and land-grabbers gathered. Within days a horde of fortune hunters was heading toward the glistening frontier in the Black Hills. They arrived in the Sioux country on horseback, in wagon trains, and on foot—some carrying only pack sacks and shovels. They prospected in the hills, along the streams, and in the mountains where the Indians hunted elk, bear, and deer. They cut down timber for campfires, staked out claims, shot the wild game for sport and food, and began building homes and starting settlements.

At first the Indians were bewildered, but they soon realized that not only were their hunting grounds being overrun but the sacred temples in the high hills where they worshiped and found health were being despoiled, and the Great Spirit was calling out for their help.

6

FROM

Cheyenne Memories

by John Stands in Timber
with Margot Liberty and Robert M. Utley

As the previous selection by Chief Red Fox illustrates, the conflict which was to erupt in the Custer battle of 1876 had, in fact, begun years before. In 1874 Custer's Seventh Cavalry had invaded the Black Hills, a sacred part of the Sioux Reservation. When Chief Red Cloud's peace treaty of 1868 was broken by this invasion, the Sioux and Cheyenne were pushed as far as they could go. Armed resistance became necessary.

In 1876 the United States Army began an organized campaign against the Sioux and Northern Cheyennes. In March of that year General George Crook fought an inconclusive battle against the Oglala Sioux led by Crazy Horse. In June hostilities recommenced. A three-pronged invasion of the Indian lands was planned by the army. On June 17, the southern prong led by General Crook was successfully countered by Crazy Horse in a fierce battle on Rosebud Creek in south-central Montana. After the engagement Crazy Horse took his warriors to the large Sioux and Cheyenne encampment on the Little Bighorn River. Proceeding according to plan, the other two prongs of the attack army, one coming from the east, and one from the west, met on the Yellowstone River and joined forces for an attack to the south. Ignorant of Crook's defeat, they intended to trap the Indians

between themselves and Crook's forces. An advance group
composed of 600 troops of Custer's Seventh Cavalry was sent
ahead as scouts. Custer discovered the Indian camp on the
Little Bighorn and attacked on June 25.

The battle which followed was ferocious. The Indians
were fighting a last stand for their homeland. Their hatred
of the white enemy was increased by the fact that several
years previously General Custer had attacked a peaceful
Cheyenne village and killed a number of unarmed women
and children in a massacre later named "The Battle of the
Washita."

The following account of the Custer fight was told by
John Stands in Timber, a Cheyenne. His story reverses the
popular myth which makes Custer a martyr and stresses in-
stead the remarkable bravery of the Indian warriors. His
account of the suicide boys at this battle is a new and im-
portant addition to the historical literature which has grown
up around the fight.

John Stands in Timber was a self-appointed historian of
the Cheyenne people. One of the last Cheyennes to learn
the tribal history from the people who had lived it, he spent
a lifetime gathering their stories in the hope that someday
they could be preserved in print. Working at assorted jobs
as a boiler tender, a farmer, and a cowboy, his real life's
work was the compilation and preservation of the tribe's
collective memory. Cheyenne Memories, written in collabora-
tion with Margot Liberty and Robert M. Utley, represents
the goal of a life's labor. John Stands in Timber died on
June 17, 1967, as his book was in press.

The attack of General George Custer on the Cheyennes and
Sioux on June 25, 1876, did not surprise the Indians as
much as many people think. They knew the soldiers were
in the country looking for them, and they expected trouble,
though they did not know just when it would come. My
grandfather, Lame White Man, told my grandmother the
morning before the fight that scouts had reported soldiers
on the Rosebud, and when they went farther down they

also saw the steamship that had brought them supplies, there in the Yellowstone River. The people of White Man Bear (or Roan Bear) were on their way to the Black Hills when they saw them. They did not turn back, but kept on their way, though they met other scouts coming this way and gave them news. It was after that that the word spread, and the Indians began gathering at the Little Horn.

But they were not ignorant on the other side either. A Crow, White Man Runs Him (one of Custer's scouts), told the Cheyennes that they were watching the Indians and each day took word to Custer of what they were doing. So each party knew pretty well where the other was.

After the main camp on the Little Horn had been established the Sioux leaders sent word that they wanted all the chiefs to gather to discuss what to do if the soldiers came. They had decided not to start anything, but to find out what the soldiers were going to do, and to talk to them if they came in peacefully. "It may be something else they want us to do now, other than go back to the reservation," they said. "We will talk to them. But if they want to fight we will let them have it, so everybody be prepared."

They also decided that the camp should be guarded by the military societies, to keep individual warriors from riding out to meet the soldiers. It was a great thing for anyone to do that—to go out and meet the enemy ahead of the rest —and they did not want this to happen. So it was agreed that both the Sioux and Cheyenne military societies would stand guard. Each society called its men, and toward evening they went on duty. Bunches of them rode to ten or fifteen stations on both sides of the river, where they could keep good watch. About sundown they could be seen, all along the hills there.

There was good reason for them to watch well. The people usually obeyed the orders of the military societies. Punishment was too severe if they did not. But that night the young men were determined to slip through. Soon after they had begun patrolling, my stepfather's friend Big Foot came to him. "Wolf Tooth," he said, "we could get away and go on through. Maybe some others will too, and meet the enemy over on the Rosebud."

They began watching to see what the military societies were doing, and to make plans. They saw a bunch of them start across to the east side of the river and another bunch on the hill between the Reno and Custer battlefields. Many more were on the high hills at the mouth of Medicine Tail Creek. So they decided what to do. After sundown they took their horses way up on the west side of the river and hobbled them, pretending to be putting them there so they could get them easily in the morning. Then they returned to camp. But when it was dark they walked back out there and got the horses, and went back down to the river. When they did they heard horses crossing and were afraid to go ahead. But the noise died away, and they went on into the river slowly, so even the water would splash more quietly. They got safely to the other side and hid in the brush all night there so they would not be discovered.

In the meantime, there was some excitement in the camp. Some of the Sioux boys had just announced that they were taking the suicide vow, and others were putting on a dance for them at the end of the camp. This meant they were throwing their lives away—they would fight till they were killed in the next battle. The Cheyennes had originated the suicide vow. Then the Sioux learned it from them, and they called this dance put on to announce it "Dying Dancing." A few Cheyenne boys had announced their decision to take the vow at the same time, so a lot of Cheyennes were up there in the crowd watching. Spotted Elk and Crooked Nose are two who remembered that night and told me about it. Both of them have been dead for a long time now. They said the people were already gathering, early in the evening. By the time they got to the upper end there a big place had been cleared and they were already dancing. When those boys came in they could not hear themselves talk, there was so much noise, with the crowd packed around and both the men and women singing.

They do not remember how many took part and never

thought of counting them, but Spotted Elk said later there were not more than twenty. They remembered the Cheyenne boys that were dancing: Little Whirlwind, Cut Belly, Closed Hand, and Noisy Walking. They were all killed the next day. None of them knew for sure that night that the soldiers were coming next day. They were just suspicious.

The next morning the Indians held a parade for the boys who had been in the suicide dance the night before. Different ones told me about it. One was my grandmother Twin Woman, the wife of Lame White Man, the only Cheyenne chief who was killed in the battle. It was customary to put on such a parade after a suicide dance. The boys went in front, with an old man on either side announcing to the public to look at these boys well; they would never come back after the next battle. They paraded down through the Cheyenne camp on the inside and back on the outside, and then returned to their own village.

While the parade was still going on, three boys went down to the river to swim—William Yellow Robe, Charles Head Swift, and Wandering Medicine. They were down there in the water when they heard a lot of noise and thought the parade had just broken up. Some riders in war clothes came along the bank yelling and shooting. Then somebody hollered at them, "The camp is attacked by soldiers!" So they never thought about swimming anymore. They jumped out and ran back to their families' camps. Head Swift's had already run away toward the hills on the west side, but his older brother came back after him. They had to run quite a distance to get his brother's horse. Then they rode double to join the women and children where they were watching the beginning of the fight. . . .

Meanwhile, after the parade ended my grandmother said a man named Tall Sioux had put up a sweat lodge, and Lame White Man went over to take part in his sweat bath there. Is was just a little way from the tepees. She said they had closed the cover down a couple of times—they usually did it four times in all, pouring water on the hot stones to make steam—and the second or third time the excitement started in the valley above the village.

She did not see which way the soldiers came, but there were some above the village. And some more came from straight across the river.

The men in the sweat tepee crawled out and ran to help their families get on their horses and get away. Lame White Man did not have time to get war clothes on. He just wrapped a blanket around his waist and grabbed his moccasins and belt and a gun. He went with Grandmother a little way to the west of some small hills there. Then he turned down below and crossed after the rest of the warriors.

Wolf Tooth and Big Foot had come out of the brush long before then. At daylight they could see the Indian military patrols still on the hills, so they waited for some time. They moved along, keeping under cover, until they ran into more warriors and then some more. Close to fifty men had succeeded in slipping through and crossing the river that way. They got together below the creek that comes in north of the present Highway 212 and were about halfway up a wooded hill there when they heard someone hollering. Wolf Tooth looked back and saw a rider on a ridge a mile below them, calling and signaling them to come back.

They turned and galloped back, and when they drew near, the rider began talking in Sioux. Big Foot could understand it. The soldiers had already ridden down toward the village. Then this party raced back up the creek again to where they could follow one of the ridges to the top, and when they got there they saw the last few soldiers going down out of sight toward the river—Custer's men. Reno's men had attacked the other end already, but they did not know it yet.

As the soldiers disappeared, Wolf Tooth's band split up. Some followed the soldiers, and the rest went on around a point to cut them off. They caught up there with some that were still going down, and came around them on both sides. The soldiers started shooting. It was the first skirmish of the battle, and it did not last very long. The Indians said they did not try to go in close. After some shooting both bunches of Indians retreated back to the hills, and the soldiers crossed the south end of the ridge where the monument now stands.

The soldiers followed the ridge down to the present cemetery site. Then this bunch of forty or fifty Indians came out by the monument and started shooting down at them again. But they were moving on down toward the river, across from the Cheyenne camp. Some of the warriors there had come across, and they began firing at the soldiers from the brush in the river bottom. This made the soldiers turn north, but they went back in the direction they had come from, and stopped when they got to the cemetery site. And they waited there a long time—twenty minutes or more.

The Indians have a joke about it. Beaver Heart said that when the scouts warned Custer about the village he laughed and said, "When we get to that village I'm going to find the Sioux girl with the most elk teeth on her dress and take her along with me." So that was what he was doing those twenty minutes, looking.

Hanging Wolf was one of the warriors who crossed the river and shot from the brush when Custer came down to the bottom. He said they hit one horse down there, and it bucked off a soldier, but the rest took him along when they retreated north. More Cheyennes and Sioux kept crossing all the time as the soldiers moved back up toward the top. Hanging Wolf thought they could have gone back between the river and the top of the ridge and made it back to Reno. But they waited too long. It gave many more warriors a chance to get across and up behind the big ridge where the monument stands, to join Wolf Tooth and the others up there.

Wolf Tooth and his band of warriors had moved in, meanwhile, along the ridge above the soldiers. Custer went into the center of a big basin below the monument, and the soldiers of the gray horse company got off their horses and moved up afoot. If there had not been so many Indians on the ridge above they might have retreated over that way, either then or later when the fighting got bad, and gone to join Reno. [Major Marcus Reno whose battalion attacked the south end of the Indian camp.] But there were too many up above, and the firing was getting heavy from the other side also.

Most of the Cheyennes were down at the Custer end of the fight, but one or two were up at the Reno fight with the Sioux. Beaver Heart saw Reno's men come in close to the village and make a stand there in some trees after they had crossed the river. But they were almost wiped out. They got on their horses and galloped along the edge of the cotton-wood trees on the bank and turned across the river, but it was a bad crossing. The bank on the other side was higher and the horses had to jump to get on top. Some fell back when it got wet and slick from the first ones coming out, and many soldiers were killed, trying to get away. Some finally made it up onto the hill—the one that is called Reno Hill today—where they took their stand.

It was about that time that Custer was going in at the lower end, toward the Cheyenne camp. It was hard work to keep track of everything at the two battles. A number of Indians went back and forth between the two, but none of them saw everything. Most of them went toward the fight with Custer, once Reno was up on the hill. Wolf Tooth said they were all shooting at the Custer men from the ridge, but they were careful all the time, taking cover. Before long some Sioux came along behind the line calling in the Sioux language to get ready and watch for the suicide boys. They said they were getting ready down below to charge together from the river, and when they came in all the Indians up above should jump up for hand-to-hand fighting. That way the soldiers would not have a chance to shoot, but be crowded from both sides.

The idea was that the soldiers had been firing both ways. When the suicide boys came up they would turn toward them, and give those behind a chance to come in close. The criers called out those instructions twice. Most of the Cheyennes could not understand them, but the Sioux there told them what had been said.

So the suicide boys were the last Indians to enter the fight. Wolf Tooth said they were really watching for them, and at last they rode out down below. They galloped up to the level ground near where the museum now is. Some turned and stampeded the gray horses of the soldiers. By then they were mostly loose, the ones that had not been shot. The rest charged right in at the place where the soldiers were making their stand, and the others followed them as soon as they got the horses away.

The suicide boys started the hand-to-hand fighting, and all of them were killed or mortally wounded. When the soldiers started shooting at them, the Indians above with Wolf Tooth came in from the other side. Then there was no time for them to take aim or anything. The Indians were right behind and among them. Some started to run along the edge under the top of the ridge, and for a distance they scattered, some going on one side and some the other. But they were all killed before they got far.

At the end it was quite a mess. They could not tell which was this man or that man, they were so mixed up. Horses were running over the soldiers and over each other. The fighting was really close, and they were shooting almost any way without taking aim. Some said it made it less dangerous than fighting at a distance. Then the soldiers would aim carefully and be more likely to hit you. After they emptied their pistols this way there was no time to reload. Neither side did. But most of the Indians had clubs or hatchets, while the soldiers just had guns. They were using these to hit with and knock the enemy down. A Sioux, Stinking Bear, saw one Indian charge a soldier who had his gun by the barrel, and he swung it so hard he knocked the Indian over and fell over himself. . . .

After the suicide boys came in it didn't take long—half an hour perhaps. Many have agreed with what Wolf Tooth

said: that if it had not been for the suicide boys it might
have ended the way it did at the Reno fight. There the
Indians all stayed back and fought. No suicide boys jumped
in to begin the hand-to-hand fight. The Custer fight was
different because those boys went in that way, and it was
their rule to be killed.

Another thing many of the Cheyennes said was that if
Custer had kept going—if he had not waited there on the
ridge so long—he could have made it back to Reno. But
probably he thought he could stand off the Indians and win.

Everyone always wants to know who killed Custer. I have
interpreted twice for people asking about this, and whether
anyone ever saw a certain Indian take a shot and kill him.
But they always denied it. Too many people were shooting.
Nobody could tell whose bullet killed a certain man. There
were rumors some knew but would not say anything for fear
of trouble. But it was more like Spotted Blackbird said: "If
we could have seen where each bullet landed we might have
known. But hundreds of bullets were flying that day."

There are all kinds of stories though. I even heard that some
Sioux had a victory dance that night, and some Cheyennes
that went over there said they saw Custer's head stuck on a
pole near the fire! They were having a big time over that
head. But the other story is, the body was not even scalped.
Anyway they are all gone now, and if anyone did know it
is too late to find out.

After they had killed every soldier, my grandmother's
brother Tall Bull came across and said, "Get a travois fixed.
One of the dead is my brother-in-law, and we will have to go
over and get his body." It was my grandfather, Lame White
Man. So they went across to where he was lying. He did not
have his war clothes on. As I said, he had not had time.
And some Sioux had made a mistake on him. They thought
he was an Indian scout with Custer—they often fought un-
dressed that way. And his scalp was gone from the top of his
head. Nearby was the body of another Cheyenne, Noisy
Walking. They were the only ones to have the places marked
where they were found.

Lame White man was the oldest Cheyenne killed, and the only Cheyenne chief. I heard that the Sioux lost sixty-six and the Cheyennes just seven, but there might have been more. The Indian dead were all moved from the battlefield right away. Four Cheyennes had been killed outright and the others badly wounded. Two died that night and one the next day. These were the dead: my grandfather; Noisy Walking, the son of White Bull or Ice; Roman Nose, the son of Long Roach; Whirlwind, the son of Black Crane; Limber Bones; Cut Belly; and Closed Hand. Closed Hand, Cut Belly, Noisy Walking, and Whirlwind had been suicide boys. They were all young men.

The Cheyenne dead were buried on the other side of the river, near where the railroad tracks now run. Some said the ones who died later, after the battle, were taken up to a place near the forks of Reno Creek several miles east of the river. We looked around there once and found one old-fashioned grave, with hides and pillows made of deer hair, and room enough under the sand rock for two or three bodies. It might have been the place. Someone had moved the rock, and a lot of stuff was lying outside there, and some human bones. . . .

Many Indians were up on the battlefield after it was over, getting the dead or taking things from the soldiers. I never heard who damaged the bodies up there. I asked many of them, and most said they did not go. A few said they had seen others doing it. They did scalp some of the soldiers, but I don't think they took the scalps into camp. The ones who had relatives killed at Sand Creek [in 1864 the Colorado militia had slaughtered 300 Cheyennes who were camped peacefully at Sand Creek] came out and chopped the heads and arms off, and things like that. They took what they wanted, coats and caps—the never used pants or shoes. Some claimed they never touched them while others said they took things. But those who had relatives at Sand Creek might have done plenty.

I asked Grandmother if she went. Women were up there as well as men. But she said the fight was still going on up above with Reno, and many women were afraid to go near the field. They thought the soldiers might break away and come in their direction. She was busy anyway, with my grandfather's body. . . .

Wandering Medicine, who was a boy then, told how he and other boys searched some of the soldiers' pockets. That square green paper money was in them, and some lying around on the ground. So they took some. Later when they were making mud horses they used it for saddle blankets. And silver money was found too. The Cheyennes made buckles out of it. They pounded it with heavy iron to flatten it out and made holes on each side, or they would string pieces together and use them for hair ornaments or necklaces, or put them on bridles as Limpy's father did.

They cut up some of the uniforms they took from the soldiers and made leggings of them. Some they just wore for coats and jackets. And they took other things. Wolf Tooth had the top of a boot cut off and sewed to make a bag. He had pliers and reloaders for a gun in that bag, and they were put away in his grave when he was buried out in the hills. I rode close to his grave a few years ago and went over and looked for it. Someone must have taken it, though I found some shells nearby. And I saw a saddle owned by one old man who had been at the battle. It was old-time Indian style, but the stirrups had come from a soldier's saddle. And some of them got canteens and guns and shells. . . .

They should mark more places on the battlefield, from the Indian side. They told me some of the stories over and over for many years, and remembered where things happened. I have marked many of the places myself with stones, but it's getting harder for me to find them now. I have tried to show other people the places so they would not be forgotten, and tell them what happened there. One is at the Reno field where a young Sioux boy charged the soldier line and was killed, following an older warrior. He was the one who lost his brother in the Rosebud fight and did not want to live any longer.

Another is where Low Dog, a Sioux, and Little Sun killed

a soldier. They had been back and forth between the two fights. They were just leaving the Reno fight to go down toward Custer when one soldier on a fast horse came from Custer's direction toward Reno Hill. They tried to head him off, but he got through them, so they turned to chase him. When they crossed Medicine Tail Coulee, Low Dog jumped off his horse. He was a good shot. He sat down to take good aim, and fired and knocked the rider off as he was going over a little knoll. Then two or three Sioux came by and took after the horse, but Little Sun did not see whether they caught it.

The big camp broke up the next day after the battle. Some people even left that evening, to move up near Lodge Grass. Some of the warriors stayed behind to go on fighting with Reno, but they did not stay more than a day. They knew that other soldiers were in the country, and they were out of meat and firewood. The camp was too big to stay together for long. They split into many groups, some following the river and others going up Reno Creek, and to other places.

My grandmother was with the Cheyennes who went toward Lodge Grass. She told a funny story of what happened there. They were camped on a big flat, some Cheyennes and some Sioux. And the Sioux dressed up soldier-style in the things they had captured, and held a parade. They were just having fun, showing off. They had a bugle. You could hear them blowing it before they reached the camp. And they had captured some of the gray horses, maybe ten or fifteen, after the suicide boys went in and stampeded them. They rode all these grays in a line carrying a flag. One was my grandmother's. White Elk had borrowed one of her horses for the battle, so he gave her one of the two grays he captured. When they had this parade, the Sioux came over and borrowed him for awhile.

Those fellows made quite a sight. Spotted Hawk told about it too. They came down along the camp in line, wearing the blue uniforms and soldiers' hats on their heads with the flag and the bugle and the gray horses. But none of them had pants on. They had no use for pants.

The parade was in the morning. They had a victory dance that night. They had a fine time. The next day they moved on again, to hunt and gather wild fruit and get ready for winter. . . .

By the time the other soldiers got to the battlefield the Indians were gone. A Cheyenne named Lost Leg rode back a few days later looking for horses. A lot of them had strayed away and they thought they might be able to get some of them. They said they could smell the battlefield a long way off. They had planned to go in and look at it, but they could not even come close, it was so strong.

So they gave up and returned another way to Reno Creek and met some of the Cheyennes moving up that way.

There was no more real fighting that summer.

7

FROM

The Way to Rainy Mountain

by N. Scott Momaday

Genocide is defined as "the use or a user of deliberate, systematic measures toward the extermination of a racial, political, or cultural group." Genocide can be effected in many ways. Mass murder by gun, bombing, or gas chamber, prolonged warfare in which one side has superior weapons and forces: these are the more obvious forms of genocide. The white man has utilized both obvious and subtle modes of committing genocide against the native peoples of America.

Large scale slaughters of unprotected Indian people, such as the massacres at Wounded Knee, Sand Creek, and the Washita River, are the most manifest genocidal atrocities committed against the Indians. Less patent, but equally deadly, has been the enclosure of Indians on reservations, consigning them to a life of poverty, disease, alcoholism, and suicide. An even less obvious but effective form of genocide practiced by the whites has been the destruction of Indian religion. For a people whose communal life evolves from a strong religious core, loss of that religion becomes genocide.

This was the form of death that the white man accorded to the Kiowa people. Originally a hunting tribe inhabiting the mountains of western Montana, the Kiowas began a long immigration south and east during the late seventeenth century. During the journey they were befriended by the Crows from whom they acquired the culture and the religion of the Plains. "They acquired horses, and their ancient nomadic spirit was suddenly free of the ground. They acquired Taime, the sacred Sun Dance Doll, from that moment the object and symbol of their worship, and so shared in the divinity of the sun. Not least they acquired the sense of destiny, therefore courage and pride. When they entered upon the southern Plains they had been transformed. No longer were they slaves to the simple necessity of survival; they were a lordly and dangerous society of fighters and thieves, hunters and priests of the sun (The Way to Rainy Mountain)."

This golden age of the Kiowas lasted for two hundred years until the hoards of white civilization invaded the southern Plains. Weakened by an epidemic of Asian cholera which destroyed half of the tribal population, the Kiowas steadily fought the United States military until 1867. In that year the majority of Kiowas were settled on reservations in the Oklahoma Indian Territory. However, white invaders again provoked the Kiowa chiefs into renewed hostilities which continued until 1875.

By 1879 the buffalo were virtually gone from the southern Plains. The Kiowas had lost their land, now they had lost their primary food source. The greatest blow to the existence of the Kiowas as a people was yet to come. In 1890 the U.S. government forbade the worship of the Sun Dance. Their source of strength and peoplehood, their link to the divine, was taken from the Kiowas. The white man had completed his program of genocide.

In the following sketch by N. Scott Momaday this tragic history of the Kiowas is revealed through the life and death of one woman, the author's grandmother. In her sorrow is seen the sorrow of an entire people; in her death is seen the death of a people.

My grandmother had a reverence for the sun, a holy regard that now is all but gone out of mankind. There was a wariness in her, and an ancient awe. She was a Christian in her later years, but she had come a long way about, and she never forgot her birthright. As a child she had been to the Sun Dances; she had taken part in those annual rites, and by them she had learned the restoration of her people in the presence of Tai-me. She was about seven when the last Kiowa Sun Dance was held in 1887 on the Washita River above Rainy Mountain Creek. The buffalo were gone. In order to consummate the ancient sacrifice—to impale the head of a buffalo bull upon the medicine tree—a delegation of old men journeyed into Texas, there to beg and barter for an animal from the Goodnight herd. She was ten when the Kiowas came together for the last time as a living Sun Dance culture. They could find no buffalo; they had to hang an old hide from the sacred tree. Before the dance could begin, a company of soldiers rode out from Fort Sill under orders to disperse the tribe. Forbidden without cause the essential act of their faith, having seen the wild herds slaughtered and left to rot upon the ground, the Kiowas backed away forever from the medicine tree. That was July 20, 1890, at the great bend of the Washita. My grandmother was there. Without bitterness, and for as long as she lived, she bore a vision of deicide.

Now that I can have her only in memory, I see my grandmother in the several postures that were peculiar to her: standing at the wood stove on a winter morning and turning meat in a great iron skillet; sitting at the south window, bent above her beadwork, and afterwards, when her vision failed, looking down for a long time into the fold of her hands; going out upon a cane, very slowly as she did when the weight of age came upon her; praying. I remember her most often at prayer. She made long, rambling prayers out of suffering and hope, having seen many things. I was never sure that I had the right to hear, so exclusive were they of all mere custom and company. The last time I saw her she prayed standing by the side of her bed at night, naked to the waist, the light of a kerosene lamp moving upon her dark skin. Her long, black hair, always drawn and braided in the day, lay upon her shoulders and against her breasts like a shawl. I do not speak Kiowa, and I never understood her prayers, but there was something inherently sad in the sound, some merest hesitation upon the syllables of sorrow. She began in a high and descending pitch, exhausting her breath to silence; then again and again—and always the same intensity of effort, of something that is, and is not, like urgency in the human voice. Transported so in the dancing light among the shadows of her room, she seemed beyond the reach of time. But that was illusion; I think I knew then that I should not see her again.

Houses are like sentinels in the plain, old keepers of the weather watch. There, in a very little while wood takes on the appearance of great age. All colors wear soon away in the wind and rain, and then the wood is burned gray and the grain appears and the nails turn red with rust. The windowpanes are black and opaque; you imagine there is nothing within, and indeed there are many ghosts, bones given up to the land. They stand here and there against the sky, and you approach them for a longer time than you expect. They belong in the distance; it is their domain.

Once there was a lot of sound in my grandmother's house, a lot of coming and going, feasting and talk. The summers there were full of excitement and reunion. The Kiowas are a summer people; they abide the cold and keep to themselves, but when the season turns and the land becomes warm and vital, they cannot hold still; an old love of going returns upon them. The aged visitors who came to my grandmother's house when I was a child were made of lean and leather, and they bore themselves upright. They wore great black hats and bright ample shirts that shook in the wind. They rubbed fat upon their hair and wound their braids with strips of colored cloth. Some of them painted their faces and carried the scars of old and cherished enmities. They were an old council of warlords, come to remind and be reminded of who they were. Their wives and daughters served them well. The women might indulge themselves; gossip was at once the mark and compensation of their servitude. They made loud and elaborate talk among themselves, full of jest and gesture, fright and false alarm. They went abroad in fringed and flowered shawls, bright bead-work and German silver. They were at home in the kitchen, and they prepared meals that were banquets.

There were frequent prayer meetings, and great nocturnal feasts. When I was a child I played with my cousins out-side, where the lamplight fell upon the ground and the singing of the old people rose up around us and carried away into the darkness. There were a lot of good things to eat, a lot of laughter and surprise. And afterwards, when the quiet returned, I lay down with my grandmother and could hear the frogs away by the river and feel the motion of the air!

Now there is a funeral silence in the rooms, the endless wake of some final word. The walls have closed in upon my grandmother's house. When I returned to it in the mourning, I saw for the first time in my life how small it was. It was late at night, and there was a white moon, nearly full. I sat for a long time on the stone steps by the kitchen door. From there I could see out across the land; I could see the long row of trees by the creek, the low light upon the rolling plains, and the stars of the Big Dipper. Once I looked at the moon and caught sight of a strange thing. A cricket had perched upon the handrail, only a few inches away from me. My line of vision was such that the creature filled the moon like a fossil. It had gone there, I thought, to live and die, for there, of all places, was its small definition made whole and eternal. A warm wind rose up and purled like the longing within me.

IV

The Indian in the Twentieth Century

"They have assumed the names and gestures of their enemies, but have held on to their own, secret souls; and in this there is a resistance and an overcoming, a long outwaiting."

N. Scott Momaday
from *House Made of Dawn*

In the nineteenth century the Indian resisted the incursion of the whites with guns and arrows. Though valiant, their struggle was doomed. By the turn of the century their numbers were decimated by war and disease, their lands stolen, their religion outlawed. The whites had conquered the continent.

As the twentieth century opened, the Indians were faced with many new problems. The disappearance of the buffalo (effected by white hunters and traders by 1879) and the loss of land had rendered their previous lifestyles impossible. The reservations they were forced to occupy possessed meager resources. Their land, water, fishing and mineral rights were (and continue to be) abrogated at will by the federal and state governments. While the standard of living rose astronomically for white society during the twentieth century, the Indians were consigned to a life of poverty.

According to data gathered by the 1950 census, the economic situation of the American Indian is the worst of any minority group in the country. Of the approximately 571,824 Indians in America, 308,103 live on reservations (figures of Robert Thomas and Samuel Stanley, University of Chicago, 1950). For most Indians on these reservations living conditions are squalid, worse than conditions in America's urban slums. Unemployment statistics of 70 percent are not unusual and on some reservations unemployment is even greater. The incidence of disease and alcoholism is very great. Many homes on reservations are not more than huts, lacking running water and sanitation facilities.

Not only is life poorer for the Indian than for all other people in America, it is also shorter. Infant death rates for American Indians are twice those of the general population. In 1969 the average age at death among the entire American population was 71 years; for the American Indian only 44 years.

Equally damaging to the collective life of the Indian in America during the twentieth century has been the government's press for total assimilation into white society. From the beginning of the century Indian children have been sent away to government boarding schools to be taught to become white. In the 1950s "relocation" became a government policy. Under this program Indians were shipped to the cities to assimilate and disappear.

These are the problems with which the writers represented in the following section are concerned, the problems which affected their lives. Helen Sekaquaptewa was kidnapped as a child and taken to government boarding schools. In his poem James Welch describes the destitute life on a Blackfoot reservation. Asa Bazhonoodah tells of the ruination of her land by strip mining for coal.

In the second half of the twentieth century there has been a growing articulation by Indians of their own needs and rights. National organizations such as the National Congress of American Indians and the National Indian Youth Council have been established. Tribal and inter-tribal groups have sprung up. Conferences and pow-wows are held throughout the country. Tribal newspapers are flourishing. While the specific proposals of these groups may vary, it is their common goal to assert their cultural and legal independence as Indians and to work for a better life for their people. Articles by and about these "new Indians," as journalist Stan Steiner has dubbed them, are included in the latter portion of this section.

1

"Indian Love Letter"

by Soge Track

The white man has torn the Indian from his own culture, demanding and enforcing assimilation. Even their native religions have been taken from the American Indians. In the sixteenth and seventeenth centuries missionaries accompanied the European explorers and settlers in America. The Indians' conversion to the Catholic faith often occurred at swordpoint. The United States government continued the shameful history of religious repression of the Indian. In 1890 the American government prohibited the practice of the Sun Dance. In the ecstatic worship of the Sun Dance ignorant white observers saw the threat of an Indian outbreak. The U.S. Army was called in and guns used to destroy both the Indians and their religion.

Thus, change was forced upon the Indian. The cultural distinctions which preserve a people were taken from them. In the following poem a young Indian considers these events, addressing her prayer to the ancient spirit of the moon. Asking for forgiveness for the people who have left the old ways, the poetess pledges not to change.

The poem was written while Soge Track was a student at the Institute of American Indian Art in Santa Fe, New

Mexico. It was published in The Writer's Reader, *the Institute's literary magazine, in 1968.*

Lady of the crescent moon
tonight I look at the sky
You are not there
"You are not mad at me, are you?
"You are angry at the people,
"Yes, I know."

　　　　they are changing
　　　　be not too hard

If you were taken to
the mission school,
not because you wanted,
but someone thought it best for you
you too would change.

They came out of nowhere
telling us how to eat our food
how to build our homes
how to plant our crops.
Need I say more of what they did?
All is new—the old ways are nothing.

　　　　they are changing
　　　　be not too hard

I talk to them
they turn their heads.
Do not be hurt—you have me
I live by the old ways
I will not change.

Tonight—my prayer plumes in hand
with the white shell things—
to the silent place I will go
(It is for you I go, please be there.)
Oh! Lady of the crescent moon
With the corn-silk hair—I love you

       they are changing
       be not too hard

2

FROM

Me and Mine,
The Life Story of Helen Sekaquaptewa
As Told to Louise Udall

Educational programs set up by whites for American Indians have always been programs to educate the Indian to the ways of the white man. During the early years of white settlement, Indian children were taken into private homes and placed in day schools by their adoptive parents.

In the early nineteenth century Congress began allotting funds "to promote civilization among the aborigines." A congressional act of March, 1819, allowed that, "The president may, in every case where he shall judge improvements in the habits and conditions of such Indians practical, and that the means of instruction can be introduced with their own consent, employ capable persons of good moral character to instruct them in the mode of agriculture suited to their situation; and for teaching their children in reading, writing, and arithmetic . . ."

This act remains the basic authorization for the educational activities carried out by the government in regard to the Indian people. Its fundamental philosophy is that the condition of the Indian be improved and corrected by a superior white father.

Unfortunately, while this paternalistic, colonialistic attitude endured, the more beneficent stipulations of this act did not. By the later nineteenth century teachers were appointed by Indian Service agents, who were themselves political appointees. Teaching positions became rewards of the patronage system and many teachers were totally incompetent.

In 1878 when government boarding schools were initiated for the training of the Indians, children were taken great distances from their homes and stripped of their customs, their language, their clothes, their very identities. Much pressure was applied to the parents to yield their children to the whites, and in some cases the children were virtually kidnapped from their homes and taken away to school under military escort.

These boarding schools were based on the model of the manual labor school which was popular in the second half of the nineteenth century. Academic instruction was combined with physical labor which supported the school and often, its white administrators also. According to Harold E. Fey and D'Arcy McNickle, authors of Indians and Other Americans:

> To this basic pattern (of the manual labor school) were added military discipline and the complete regimentation of the child's waking hours. Moreover, the schools were dedicated to the ultimate eradication of all traits of Indian culture. The location of the schools at distances far removed from the reservations from which children were selected was deliberate policy. Children were often no more than five or six years old when they arrived at these schools. If the child could be taken young enough and moved far enough away from the influences of family and tribe, the odds against his ever again becoming part of his environment were remote.

Indian resistance to this kind of schooling is understandable. Though the day school was less drastic in its effect of disassociating the Indian child from his culture, it, too, was hated and resisted.

The following selection by Helen Sekaquaptewa tells of the conspiracy of Hopi parents and children to elude the police officials who came to take the youth away to school. Although made into a game, this conflict represented real resistance to assimilation.

Helen Sekaquaptewa was born in the village of Oraibi, one of eleven independent Hopi villages in the arid plateau area of northeastern Arizona. As a young girl she was a captive student in the day school described below. Later, she was forced to attend the Keams Canyon boarding school. Her education was concluded at a secondary school in Phoenix. Her later life was spent on a Hopi reservation where she managed to retain some of the tribal customs while living the life she learned at school.

The dictation of Me *and* Mine *was completed in 1968 and was published the following year.*

When we were five or six years of age, we, with our parents became involved with the school officials, assisted by the Navajo policemen, in a serious and rather desperate game of hide-and-seek, where little Hopi boys and girls were the forfeit in the game. Every day the school principal sent out a truant officer, and many times he himself went with the officer, going to Hopi homes to take the children to school. The Navajo policemen who assisted in finding hidden children were dressed in old army uniforms, and they wore cavalry hats over their long hair, done up in a knot. This made quite a picture—especially the traditional hair style with a white man's hat. It had not been customary for Indians to wear hats up to that time.

When September came there was no peace for us. Early in the morning, from our houses on the mesa, we could see the principal and the officer start out from the school, walking up the trail to "get" the children. Hostile parents tried every day in different ways to hide us from them, for once you were caught, you had lost the game. You were discovered and listed and you had to go to school and not hide any more. I was finally caught and went to the Oraibi day school one session, when I was about six years old, but not before many times outwitting Mr. Schoolman.

Sometimes, after a very early breakfast, somebody's grandmother would take a lunch and go with a group of eight to twelve little girls and hide them in the cornfields away out from the village. On another day another grandmother would go in the other direction over the hills among the cedars where we would play in a ravine, have our lunch and come back home in the afternoon. Men would be out with little boys playing this game of hide-and-seek. One day I got left behind and was sent out with a group of boys. I didn't know the man, and the boys' games were not for me, and I cried all day.

A place where one or two small children could be stowed away on short notice was the rabbit blanket. A rabbit blanket is made by cutting dressed rabbit skins in two-inch strips and weaving them into a warp of wool thread. When not in use, in warm weather, this blanket is hung by the four corners from a hook in the rafter beam, to prevent it from being moth-eaten. But once discovered, this hiding place was out. The school officer would feel of the rabbit blanket first thing on coming into the room.

Most houses have a piki [a maize bread, made in thin, paperlike sheets] storage cupboard in a partition wall. This would be the thickness of the wall and about two by three feet. A cloth covered the front, making a good place to keep the piki supply dry and clean. One day the officers were only two doors away when my mother was aware of their presence. She snatched her young son Henry and put him curled up in the piki cupboard just in time to win the game—that day.

Our houses were two and three stories high. When a lower room became old and unsafe, it was used as a dump place for ashes, peach stones, melon and squash seeds, and bits of discarded corn; anything that could be eaten was preserved in the ashes, and the room was gradually filled. Then in time of famine these bits of food could be dug out and eaten. In the home of my childhood such a room was about three-fourths filled. One September morning my brother and I were hidden there. We lay on our stomachs in the dark, facing a small opening. We saw the feet of the principal and policeman as they walked by, and heard their big voices as they looked about wondering where the children were. They didn't find us that day.

One morning an older man took several boys out to hide. Emory, who was later my husband, was one of these boys. The man took them off the mesa where there was a big fissure in a sheer cliff with a bigger space behind it, away down in the rocks where no horse could go. The grandfather told the boys to stay there and be quiet. He then went a little way away and began hoeing in an orchard. The boys soon wanted to come out and play, but the grandfather said "no." Pretty soon they heard the sound of approaching horses' hoofs and looking up to the top of the cliff saw the Navajo policeman. He rode around out of sight, but pretty soon was seen coming up the valley toward the grandfather. The policeman couldn't get into the crack in the rock but he got off his horse looking for footprints. The boys had been careful to step on rocks and grass and left no footprints. After looking around a while the policeman got on his horse and rode away. After he left and they were sure he would not come back, the boys came out to play, and later the grandfather brought out the lunch.

Some boys made trouble after they were enrolled in school. At recess they would run away. They could outrun the principal. One principal, in desperation, got himself a .22 rifle with blank bullets. When he shot at the boys they stopped running.

I don't remember for sure just how I came to be "caught." Maybe both my mother and myself got a little tired of getting up early every morning and running off to hide all day. She probably thought to herself, "Oh, let them get her. I am tired of this. It is wearing me down." The hide-and-seek game continued through September, but with October, the colder weather was on the schoolman's side.

So, one morning, I was "caught." Even then, it was the rule among mothers not to let the child go voluntarily. As the policeman reached to take me by the arm, my mother put her arm around me. Tradition required that it appear that

I was forced into school. I was escorted down off the mesa to the schoolhouse, along with several other children. First, each was given a bath by one of the Indian women who worked at the school. Baths were given in the kitchen in a round, galvanized tub. Then we were clothed in cotton underwear, cotton dresses, and long black stockings and heavy shoes, furnished by the government. Each week we had a bath and a complete change of clothing. We were permitted to wear the clothes home each day, but my mother took off the clothes of the detested white man as soon as I got home, until it was time to go to school the next day.

Names were given to each child by the school. Mine was "Helen." Each child had a name card pinned on, for as many days as it took for the teacher to learn and remember the name she had given us. Our teacher was Miss Stanley. She began by teaching us the names of objects about the room. We read a little from big charts on the wall later on, but I don't remember ever using any books. . . .

3

"Christmas Comes to Moccasin Flat"

by James Welch

James Welch knew what it was like to grow up on an American Indian reservation. He shared a life of poverty with the members of his tribe, but he also shared tribal memories of a past greatness. In the poem which follows he captures both the feeling of despair and the treasured memories which sustain his people.

James Welch was born in 1940 in Browning, Montana, on the Blackfoot Reservation. He received a Master of Arts degree in creative writing at the University of Montana. "Christmas Comes to Moccasin Flat" appeared in The Young American Poets, *edited by Paul Carroll, published in 1968.*

Christmas comes like this: wise men
unhurried, candles bought on credit (poor price
for calves), warriors face down in wine sleep.
Winds cheat to pull heat from smoke.

Friends sit in chinked cabins, stare out
plastic windows and wait for commodities.
Charlie Blackbird, twenty miles from church
and bar, stabs his fire with flint.

When drunks drain radiators for love
or need, chiefs eat snow and talk of change,
an urge to laugh pounding their ribs.
Elk play games in high country.

Medicine woman, clay pipe and twist tobacco,
calls each blizzard by name and predicts
five o'clock by spitting at her television.
Children lean into her breath to beg a story:

Something about honor and passion,
warriors back with meat and song,
a peculiar evening star, quick vision of birth.
Blackbird builds his fire. Outside, a quick thirty below.

4

FROM

The Memoirs of Chief Red Fox

By Chief William Red Fox

"A careful review of the historical literature reveals that the dominant policy of the Federal government toward the American Indian has been one of forced assimilation which has vacillated between the two extremes of coercion and persuasion. At the root of the assimiliation policy has been a desire to divest the Indian of his land and resources." (Senate Report No. 91–501, 91st Congress, 1st Session.)

To promulgate this assimilation policy the United States has passed thousands of laws regulating the relationship between the Indian and the land, and between the Indian and the white government. Vast bureaucracies have been set up to administer these laws. Unfortunately, many of these laws have had disastrous effects on the cultural and economic life of the Indian. Government bureaucracies have often created more problems than they have solved.

In the following selection Chief Red Fox considers the effects that government administration has had on the lives of American Indians. Far from being a benevolent protector, the government has sanctioned the theft of Indian resources. The government has allowed the Indian people to become a marginal population whose poverty is enforced and whose welfare is virtually ignored.

*   *   *

The Bureau of Indian Affairs was established by Congress after most of the Indians had been captured and placed upon reservations. The cavalry had assassinated their leaders and their tribes were broken up and demoralized. In all this time only one Indian has been selected to head the bureau. That was Robert Benson, who was appointed by President Johnson in 1966. He was an Oneida from Wisconsin, a career man in the bureau. From his position at the top, where complete information was accessible, he became dismayed at the government's neglect of its Indian wards who were scattered on 241 reservations across the country. His attempts to bring about reforms and improvements through Congress and other sources failed. Everywhere he encountered apathy from officials who were occupied with what they considered more pressing problems. Frustrated and discouraged, he resigned in July, 1969, stating that the administration was "completely ignoring the Indian."

About that same time Senator Edward Kennedy, chairman of the subcommittee on Indian education, said:

"Our nation's policies and programs for educating American Indians are a national tragedy."

Another senator, Walter Mondale of Minnesota, added to this by charging that the Indian schools contain the elements of disaster. "The first thing an Indian learns is that he is a loser," he declared.

Speaking in similar vein McGeorge Bundy, President of the Ford Foundation, said:

"The American Indians are by any measure, save cultural heritage, the country's most disadvantaged minority."

A few Indians who occupy places of influence in White society have added bits of criticism to fill in the picture of neglect. Among them is Vine Deloria, a Standing Rock Sioux who, in the recent book *Our Brother's Keeper,* says:

"The Indians in White America angrily indict Whites for keeping the Indian a stranger in his homeland."

The extent of the suffering and deprivation among Indians is reflected by statistics obtained from the government in 1969, which showed that their life expectancy is forty-four years compared to seventy-one for the rest of the nation's population. Their average family income is $1,500. The average schooling for an Indian child is five and a half years, which is far below that for both Black and Mexican-American children. Statistics from another bureau in Washington are equally revealing and tragic. The suicide rate among Indian teen-agers is three times the national average, and on some reservations, it is ten times as high.

The facts that underlie these statistics are clearly defined in the neglect, poverty, and hopelessness that prevail almost everywhere on the reservations. Much of the land held in trust for the Indians by the government is unproductive. The Apache reservation in Arizona is an example. That is a picture-post-card region with skyscraping mountains covered with ponderosa, valleys of unforgettable loveliness, and inhospitable deserts; but it is unsuitable for farming, and many of the Indians live there in windowless wooden shacks with corrugated metal roofs and subsist on meager supplies from the scrawny hand of welfare, and the crops grown sparsely on a sprinkling of tillable soil. The sight of an Indian woman toting pails of water, a mile or more from her shack, is common, and the cesspool prevails as a symbol of status for the inhabitants.

America's preoccupation with the world wars, a shattering depression, and a multitude of other ethnic, social, and economic problems has left little time in the twentieth century for the nation to consider how the Indians were faring. They have been a neglected, almost forgotten minority, while most Americans believe they are being fed, clothed, sheltered and, in general, coddled by a benevolent government. They number only one-four-hundredth of the population. The Negroes are ten times as numerous and much more vocal in making their needs and wants known. These two races differ in their backgrounds, ethnic traits, and aptitudes. While the Negro has become forceful in a competitive society, with oratory on his lips and a longing in his heart for equality, the Indian, developed through centuries by the adamant forces of nature, is a subdued, stoical figure.

In recent years, a faction has come to the front among Negroes urging them to maintain and perpetuate their racial and cultural identity. The leaders of this movement feel that the White man has left a vacuum that can be filled only by establishing man's identity with himself and nature. They assert that the Negro is a distinct unit in the spectrum of races and should be proud of his inheritance and achievements. This has always been fundamental in the composition of the Indian. He never bowed or fawned before the White man, or conceded superiority to his artificial culture. His faith in the Great Spirit sustained his faith in himself as an individual and welded his character to the ethical structure of morality and integrity.

There is not much intercourse between reservation Indians and the better class of White people. Race prejudice is the primary cause. There has been a trifling improvement in this attitude in recent years, but many Indians cling to their ancient customs and beliefs and this continues to set them apart from other races. Even the missionaries and teachers have been unable to convince them that White civilization is an improvement over the one developed by their ancestors. Business transactions are the main contacts between the two races. The Indians have separate churches and schools, separate fairs, dances, and community centers. Some of their children attend public schools, but even there prejudice exists, although not among officials and teachers. You can imagine a timid Indian boy of five or six years of age being greeted when he enters a public school by:

"Hi, Tonto, where's your horse?" or "Why didn't you bring your tomahawk?" Being sensitive, as all Indian children are, especially in the presence of Whites, the boy does not know how to respond and slinks into the school house, spiritually and mentally injured. There may have been no intention to ridicule him, but children are universally cruel without knowing it, and sensing that the boy is vulnerable, they continue to taunt him. An Indian boy or girl is a racial outcast in almost any elementary school among a White majority. The prejudice is inborn, and only the most perceptive teachers can eradicate it. In high school, if the Indian child gets that far, he has a better chance, for students of that age are more discerning and the virtue of compassion has developed, as a desert flower, at least in some of them.

The right to vote has not been of much benefit to the Indians. Every two years, during the heat of campaigns, both political parties manifest solicitude for them, but this disappears after the elections. The black-robed figure of injustice and the concealed hand of cruelty appeared in 1969 among the Navajos, who were reported to have been "reduced to Biafra-level malnutrition by greedy White traders and water-sponging farmers." Documented information on this was submitted to the United States Senate, and a member of that august body was shown in newspaper stories as a champion of the exploiters.

Time and again, the water resources of the Indians have been diverted to irrigate other lands, and countless acres have been confiscated for dams and public recreation parks. An example of this occurred in the 1950s when the Tuscaroras of New York had to relinquish 553 fertile acres for a reservoir. They were paid $850,000, but the Niagara University received $5,000,000 for 200 acres in the same vicinity. In 1924 the Army Corps of Engineers sliced off 10,000 acres from the Seneca Reservation for the Kinzua Dam, paying them $3,000,000 and engendering a lot of bitterness in the tribe.

The injustice that appears on the national scene shows up in minor happenings on the reservation. The inner reactions of the Indians can well be imagined when they are present at scenes like that which I witnessed in the federal court at Deadwood, South Dakota:

An Indian youth was arrested and taken before the judge for illegal possession of liquor, and he was given a jail sentence. The Indians knew that the complaining official, the executive on the reservation, had plenty of liquor in his home and his "whiskey breath" could be detected while he testified; yet he was allowed to leave the courtroom (a hallowed place, the White man told them) with an air of satisfaction in knowing that his records would show another conviction of an Indian lawbreaker. That is an example of why the Indians do not cooperate wholeheartedly with the law enforcement officers. If given the responsibility of policing themselves on their reservations, they would be on the alert to prevent and detect crime, and to create the spirit of obedience to the laws. The young people would obey their officers, and the hostility they feel toward those whom they look upon as oppressors and enemies would cease to exist.

In the spring of 1969 the Associated Press published an article about a White trader, acting as postmaster, who plucked an old woman's welfare check as it went through the mail. The story continued:

"He barged into her hogan and demanded that she endorse the check. When she refused to sign it, he brandished a knife at her. Still she resisted, and he grabbed her hand, forced her thumb on an ink pad, and then forcibly 'endorsed' the check with her thumbprint. Two outraged property crop lawyers went to the trader and threatened him with charges of assault and battery and illegal conversion. The bully returned the check and settled the assault case with an additional $100."

Americans who run away to recreation parks and seashores on weekends and vacations no doubt have a nostalgia for the wilderness, an unconscious yearning for the rugged, the cruel, the gentle, and sometimes for solitary communion with the Great Spirit; but almost everywhere they go, they leave the campsites and beaches littered with the wrappings of civilization. They find a land despoiled by bulldozers and dredges that have torn down mountains, dammed rivers, and converted the beauty spots of nature into homesites to accommodate a population that is running wild. This is called "progress," a word that should be scissored from the dictionary and replaced by "predaceous."

Most of the Indians on reservations cling to their ancient ways, but through the years, many, discomfited by government restrictions and resigned to the passing of primitive America, have moved into White society and intermarried, and their blood runs through the biological potpourri that makes the nation a composite of all the races of mankind. Some have succeeded in professions and trades, but the majority have assembled in colonies, where they live in depression and squalor. Almost 60,000 are in Los Angeles, 20,000 in San Francisco, 15,000 in Chicago's North Side. Others are congregated in timeworn apartments and shabby dwellings in Phoenix, Minneapolis, and other cities.

There are some who recoil from the crammed-in slovenliness of urban life and return to the reservations, but more are overpowered by loneliness. Nature is a worshipful reality, and they cling to its frazzled edges with enduring respect and withered hopes.

A few activists implore them to ignore demands of the past and countenance the commanding culture of the White man, but the call of the wild does not die easily in the deep rivers of biology.

I have talked to some who gave up life in the cities and returned to their families and relatives. They found the city a smothering place of smoke, factory fumes, and canned foods, and beer parlors the only place where they could find companionship.

"The land and open spaces called me back," one young man said. "I would rather sit on a river bank and mourn for the past than accept what the White man has offered me."

One of the major problems of the Indians almost everywhere is alcohol. Before the White man introduced whiskey among them, they had never tasted strong drink, but the phrase "like a drunken Indian" came into the language in the seventeenth century. The trader found that a few drinks of whiskey conditioned the Indian for selling his furs, or even his homestead, for a pittance. Even the missionaries had little success in stopping that kind of thievery. The liquor problem, however, did not become endemic until the present

century. Faced with an alien, hostile civilization, treated with
contempt, and beaten down by despair, the Indian turned to
drink as a means of escape. On one Western reservation 44
percent of the men and 21 percent of the women were arrested in one year for drunkenness. A statement by Bill Pen-
sioneau, president of the National Indian Youth Council,
amplified this:

"The only time we are free is when we are drunk."

White people who are unacquainted with the Indians and
wish to visit their reservations should take warning to never
judge the Indian's intelligence by his general appearance or
actions, since in the presence of strangers he may sit on his
horse and gaze out into space as though he had no interest
in life, yet in reality, he has studied the White man and
perhaps has a rather accurate picture of his station in life
and his personality. His keen eye and silent tongue enable
him to quickly comprehend new surroundings, a gift that
has made him an excellent hunter and a great soldier.

Then too, the Indian horseman may be thinking of how
he has been regarded as a savage for decades because that
was the only way the White man could justify his acts as he
swept across America shooting everything in his gunsights.

5

"They Are Taking the Holy Elements from Mother Earth"

by Asa Bazhonoodah

The white man has mobilized every force at his command, armies, laws, administrators, in his efforts to eradicate the Indian. Yet the Indian refuses to vanish, refuses to die for the white man. He continues to fight today to preserve his past, protect his present interests, and build for his future.

As it has in the last three centuries, the Indian's struggle continues to center upon the preservation of the land and its natural resources. New elements have arisen in the conflict between the white and the Indian over land, elements introduced by the modern and often destructive technological innovations of white civilization.

The following selection is an affidavit submitted to an Arizona court by an Apache woman, registering her opposition to the strip mining of her home, the Black Mesa. Her plea arises from a natural regard for the land which has supported her family for generations. She doesn't need scientists to inform her of the destructive effects of strip mining on the ecology of her home; she has experienced this. Perhaps she knows that the white man utilizes strip mining because it is the cheapest means of extracting solid fuel from the earth. She has seen the explosions which blast away soil, rock, and plant life to expose the raw coal. She has seen the bulldozers tearing the coal from the earth. She has seen the trucks which carry the coal to the power stations to generate energy for the whites. She has seen the wreckage of the land. And she knows that the white man doesn't care.

In English they call me "Kee Shelton's Mother." In Navajo my name is Asa Bazhonoodah, "Woman who had squaw dance." I am 84 years old.

I am originally from Black Mesa. I was born and raised there. My parents and grandparents were all from that same area.

At present I live east and not far from the mining site. I was born in a hogan which was still standing the last time I saw it. But now I don't know, maybe they have torn it down.

They tell me my parents used to live right down at the mining site at the time my mother was pregnant with me. Then when she was going to give birth to me they moved eastward to the place where I was born. This is not too far from the place they grind the coal. That is where I was raised and after I got married my husband and I lived at the same place. During that time my husband cleared land and built a fence for a cornfield near where we lived. We used to move to the cornfield to plant and harvest the corn.

My mother died and was buried right there at our permanent home. Following that my husband died during the time people were killed by some kind of disease and he also is buried there. After this happened I moved to the cornfield which my husband had established. The cornfield is still there and I plant a little bit of corn every spring.

I strongly object to the strip mining for many reasons. The mine workers do a lot of drinking and they take youngsters with them and give them liquor and wine. These are the children of my husband's grandchildren with whom we used to live.

The particles of coal dust that contaminate the water kill our animals. I know this for a fact because many of the sheep belonging to my children were killed. I have some cows and they started dying off. And now it has become too frequent, almost every day. We were asked to report every dead sheep or animal but it is impossible to do that because of the lack of communication. We don't have a trading post or a police station on Black Mesa where we could report these happenings.

We do not like the explosions at the mine because it scares our horses. Many of us herd sheep on horseback and every time an explosion goes off it scares the animals and they are afraid and try to run away.

The coal mine is destroying our grazing lands, because the grass is being put under the earth, and our sheep are getting thin, and not having many lambs. The .mine also destroys our springs and water holes, so we have great trouble trying to water our livestock. My sheep are my life. Black Mesa is my "billfold" as the white man says. Black Mesa gives life to animals and these animals give us money. The stuff I prod my donkey with is like the pencil the whites use.

A long time ago the earth was placed here for us, the people, the Navajo. It gives us corn and we consider her our mother.

When Mother Earth needs rain we give pollen and use the prayers that were given us when we came from the earth. That brings rain. Black Mesa area is used to ask for rain. And afterward (after the mining) we don't know what it will be like. We make prayers for all blessings for Mother Earth, asking that we may use her legs, her body and her spirit to make ourselves more powerful and durable. After this the pollen is thrown into the water.

Air is one of the Holy Elements, it is important in prayer. Wooded areas are being cut down. Now the air is becoming bad, not working. The herbs that are taken from Mother Earth and given to a woman during childbirth no longer grow in the cut area. The land looks burned.

The Earth is our mother. The white man is ruining our mother. I don't know the white man's ways, but to us the Mesa, the air, the water, are Holy Elements. We pray to these Holy Elements in order for our people to flourish and perpetuate the well-being of each generation.

Even when we were small, our cradle is made from the things given to us from Mother Earth. We use these elements all of our lives and when we die we go back to Mother Earth.

When we were first put on Earth, the herbs and medicine were also put here for us to use. These have become part of our prayers to Mother Earth. We should realize it for if we forget these things we will vanish as the people. This is why I don't like it. The whites have neglected and misused the Earth. Soon the Navajo will resemble the Anasazi. The wind took them away because they misused Earth. The white men wish that nothing will be left of us after his is over. They want us like the Anasazi.

Mother Earth is like a horse. We put out hay and grain to bring in the horse. So it is when we put out pollen to bring life from Mother Earth. We pray to Mother Earth to ask blessings from the water, the sun, and the moon. Why are they going up there (to the moon)? I'm also against this. This fooling around with the sacred elements.

This pollution is what I'm especially against. When I first realized I had eyes, I saw that it was clear. Now it is getting hazy and gray outside. The coal mine is causing it. Because of the bad air, animals are not well, they don't feel well. They know what is happening and are dying. Peabody Coal Company is tampering with the Holy Elements, and this must be stopped.

I don't think Peabody Coal Company can replant the land. There is nothing but rocks, no soil. I don't see how they could replant. The soil is underneath. They advocate that this place will be beautiful when they finish. I don't believe that this place will be beautiful when they finish. If they replant, they will not replant our herbs. Even now our herbs are vanishing.

I have gone three times looking for herbs. I couldn't recognize the place where we find them. Finally I found some plants but they were scorched. I couldn't find my way around the mountain because it was so disturbed by the mining operation.

We have herbs that cure diseases that white medicine doesn't cure. Sometime the people come here to find medicine when the Public Health Service doesn't cure them. They pray and give Mother Earth something for curing them. This the white people do not know about.

Our prayer and healing have been tampered with and they don't work as well anymore.

How can we give something of value to Mother Earth to repay the damages that the mining had done to her. We still ask her for blessings and healing, even when she is hurt.

They are taking water and the other Holy Elements from her veins.

I don't want highways built because stock will be run over and the children hurt.

I see the cedar trees next to the ponds they built have turned red. The grasses are dying.

I want to see them stop taking water from inside the Mesa. The water underground, which works with that water that falls to the surface of Mother Earth, will wash away.

I want to see the burial grounds left alone. All of my relatives' graves are being disturbed.

How much would you ask if your mother had been harmed? There is no way that we can be repaid for the damages to our Mother. No amount of money we repay, money cannot give birth to anything. I want to see the mining stopped.

6

Proclamation of the Indians of Alcatraz

by Indians of all Tribes, San Francisco, California

In November of 1969 fourteen Indian college students invaded the abandoned prison island of Alcatraz and reclaimed the land "by right of discovery." After nineteen hours they left, but the idea of an Indian occupation of Alcatraz caught fire.

Two weeks later a force of nearly 100 Indians returned to Alcatraz with a supply system and a great determination to stay. When the General Services Administration of the federal government gave them a deadline for leaving, they refused to go. The deadline was withdrawn. When the U.S. Coast Guard made a feeble attempt to blockade ships carrying supplies to the island, their vessel was met by a hail of arrows.

For nearly two years the Indians retained possession of Alcatraz. The island became a center for Indian culture, both a real and symbolic fortress in the Indians' fight for survival as a distinct and noble people.

The following proclamation is a statement of purpose, written by the Indians who took Alcatraz, in the name of all native Americans.

PROCLAMATION:

TO THE GREAT WHITE FATHER AND ALL HIS PEOPLE

We, the native Americans, re-claim the land known as Alcatraz Island in the name of all American Indians by right of discovery.

We wish to be fair and honorable in our dealings with the Caucasian inhabitants of this land, and hereby offer the following treaty:

We will purchase said Alcatraz Island for twenty-four dollars ($24) in glass beads and red cloth, a precedent set by the white man's purchase of a similar island about 300 years ago. We know that $24 in trade goods for these 16 acres is more than was paid when Manhattan Island was sold, but we know that land values have risen over the years. Our offer of $1.24 per acre is greater than the 47¢ per acre that the white men are now paying the California Indians for their land.

We will give to the inhabitants of this island a portion of that land for their own, to be held in trust by the American Indian Affairs and by the bureau of Caucasian Affairs to hold in perpetuity—for as long as the sun shall rise and the rivers go down to the sea. We will further guide the inhabitants in the proper way of living. We will offer them our religion, our education, our life-ways, in order to help them achieve our level of civilization and thus raise them and all their white brothers up from their savage and unhappy state. We offer this treaty in good faith and wish to be fair and honorable in our dealings with all white men.

*   *   *

We feel that this so-called Alcatraz Island is more than suitable for an Indian Reservation, as determined by the white man's own standards. By this we mean that this place resembles most Indian reservations in that:

1. It is isolated from modern facilities, and without adequate means of transportation.

2. It has no fresh running water.
3. It has inadequate sanitation facilities.
4. There are no oil or mineral rights.
5. There is no industry and so unemployment is very great.
6. There are no health care facilities.
7. The soil is rocky and non-productive; and the land does not support game.
8. There are no educational facilities.
9. The population has always exceeded the land base.
10. The population has always been held as prisoners and kept dependent upon others.

Further, it would be fitting and symbolic that ships from all over the world, entering the Golden Gate, would first see Indian land, and thus be reminded of the true history of this nation. This tiny island would be a symbol of the great lands once ruled by free and noble Indians.

7

"The Red Man's Burden"

by Peter Collier

In the following selection taken from Ramparts *magazine journalist Peter Collier presents the story of La Nada Means, one of the original occupiers of Alcatraz. While her personal history is unique, it represents the kind of life which our society offers to the young Indian: a life of denial, including the denial of Indian identity. It is this history, combined with a passionate determination not to be destroyed as an Indian person that brought La Nada together with her sisters and brothers to Alcatraz.*

Alcatraz is Indian territory: The old warning to "Keep Off U.S. Property" now reads "Keep off Indian Property;" security guards with red armbands stand near the docks to make sure it is obeyed. Women tend fires beneath huge iron cauldron filled with food, while their kids play frisbee in what was once a convicts' exercise yard. Some of the men work on the prison's wiring system or try to get more cell-blocks cleared out for the Indian people who are arriving daily from all over the country; others sit fishing on the wharf with hand-lines, watching quietly as the rip tides churn in the Bay. During the day, rock music plays over portable radios and a series of soap operas flit across a TV; at night, the prison is filled with the soft sounds of ceremonial drums and eerie songs in Sioux, Kiowa and Navajo.

In the few weeks of its occupation, Alcatraz has become a mecca, a sort of red man's Selma. Indian people come, stay a few days, and then leave, taking with them a sense of wonderment that it has happened. Middle-aged "establishment" Indians are there. They mix with younger insurgents like Lehman Brightman (the militant Sioux who heads a red power organization called the United Native Americans). Mad-Bear Anderson (the Iroquois traditionalist from upstate New York who fought to get the United Nations to stop the U.S. Army Corps of Engineers' flooding of precious Seneca Indian lands), Sid Mills (the young Yakima who demanded a discharge from the Army after returning from Viet-Nam so that he could fight his real war—against the state of Washington's denial of his people's fishing rights), and Al Bridges (one of the leaders of the first Washington fish-ins in 1964, who now faces a possible ten-year prison sentence for defying the state Fish and Game Commission). The composition of the ad hoc Indian community changes constantly, but the purpose remains the same: to make Alcatraz a powerful symbol of liberation springing out of the long American imprisonment.

The people enjoy themselves, spending a lot of time sitting around the campfire talking and gossiping. But there is a sense of urgency beneath the apparent lassitude. Richard Oakes, a 27-year-old Mohawk who worked in high steel construction before coming West to go to college, is one of the elected spokesmen. Sitting at a desk in the old Warden's Office, he talks about the hope of beginning a new organization, the Confederacy of American Indian Nations, to weld Indian groups all over the country into one body capable of taking power away from the white bureaucracy. He acknowledges that the pan-Indian movements which have sprung up before have always been crushed. "But time is running out for us," he says. "We have everything at stake. And if we don't make it now, then we'll get trapped at the bottom of that white world out there, and wind up as some kind of Jack

Jones with a social security number and that's all. Not just on Alcatraz, but every place else, the Indian is in his last stand for cultural survival."

This sentiment is reflected in the slogans lettered on walls all over the prison, the red paint bleeding down onto the concrete. One of them declares: "Better Red than Dead. . . ."

One of the original 14 on Alcatraz was a pretty 22-year-old Shoshone-Bannock girl named La Nada Means. Her hair is long and reddish-black; her nose arches slightly and prominent cheekbones square out her face. Her walk is slightly pigeon-toed, the result of a childhood disease for which she never received treatment. If you tell her that she looks very Indian, she will thank you, but with a searching look that suggests she has heard the same comment before, and not as a compliment.

"When I was little," she says, "I remember my family as being very poor. There were 12 of us kids, and we were always hungry. I remember sometimes getting to the point where I'd eat anything I could get my hands on—leaves, small pieces of wood, anything. The other thing I remember is the meanness of the small towns around the reservation. Blackfoot, Pocatello—they all had signs in the store windows to keep Indians out. One of them I'll never forget; it said, 'No Indians or Dogs Allowed.' There were Indian stalls in the public bathrooms; Indians weren't served in a lot of the restaurants; and we just naturally all sat in the balcony of the theaters. You learn early what all that means. It becomes part of the way you look at yourself."

She grew up on the Fort Hall reservation in southern Idaho. The Jim Crow atmosphere of the surrounding small towns has lessened somewhat with the passage of time and the coming of the civil-rights bills, but it is still very much present in the attitude of white townsfolk towards Indians. And while there are no longer the small outbreaks of famine that occurred on the reservation when La Nada was growing up in the '50s, Fort Hall is still one of the bleakest areas in the country, and the people there are among the poorest.

Like most Indian children of her generation (and like a great many today), La Nada Means was sent away to school. Her youth became a series of separations from home and family, each more traumatic than the one before. The first school she attended was St. Mary's School for Indian Girls in Springfield, South Dakota. "I took a lot of classes in subjects like 'Laundry,' " she remembers, "where the classwork was washing the headmaster's clothes. All Indian people are supposed to be good with their hands, you know, and also hard workers, so we didn't do too much regular schoolwork at St. Mary's. They also had what they called a Summer Home Program where you're sent out during the summer break to live with a white family. It was supposed to teach you white etiquette and things like that, and make you forget your savage Indian ways. When I was 13, I was sent up to Minnesota where I became a sort of housekeeper for the summer. I don't remember too much about it, except that the wages I got, about $5 a week, were sent back to St. Mary's and I never saw them. After being at that school a little while, I got all upset. They said I was 'too outspoken,' and expelled me. After I got back to Fort Hall, I had my first breakdown."

For awhile she attended public school in Blackfoot, the small town bordering the reservation. She was suspended because she objected to the racial slurs against Indians which were built into the curriculum. She was 15 when the Bureau of Indian Affairs (BIA) sent her to its boarding school in Chilocco, Oklahoma. On her first day there, the matrons ordered her to lower the hems on the two dresses she owned. She refused and was immediately classified as a troublemaker. "At Chilocco, you're either a 'good girl' or 'a bad girl,' " she says. "They put me in the bad girls' dormitory right away with Indians mainly from the Northwest. The Oklahoma Indians were in the good girls' dorm, and the matrons constantly tried to keep us agitated by setting the tribes to fighting with each other. Everything was like the Army. There were bells, drills and set hours for everything. The food was called 'GI Chow.' There was a lot of brutality, but it was used mainly on the boys, who lived in another wing. Occasionally they'd let the boys and girls get together. You all stood in this big square; you could hold hands, but if the matrons saw you getting too close, they'd blow a whistle and then you'd have to march back to the dorm."

La Nada made the honor roll, but was expelled from Chilocco after a two-month stay for being involved in a fight. "The matrons just had it in for me, I guess. They got about 100 other Indian girls against me and a few other 'bad girls.' They put us in a small room and when the fight was ready to begin, they turned out the lights and walked out, locking the doors behind them. We had a 'riot,' and I got beat up. The next day, the head of the school called me into his office and said that I didn't fit in."

She was sent off with one dollar, a sack of lunch, and a one-way bus ticket from Chilocco back to Idaho. She lived with her family for a few months, helping her father collect data about conditions at Fort Hall, and then was sent by the BIA to another of its boarding schools, Stewart Institute, in Carson City, Nevada. Her reputation as a "difficult Indian" followed her, and she was again sent home after being at Stewart for less than a day. The BIA threatened to send her to "reform" school; then it forgot about her. "I stayed around the reservation for awhile," she says, "and when I got to be 17, I took GED (high school equivalent) exams. I only had about nine real years of schooling, but I scored pretty well and got into Idaho State College. I lasted there for a semester and then quit. I didn't really know what to do. At Fort Hall, you either work in some kind of menial job with the BIA agency there, or you go off the reservation to find a job in one of the towns. If you choose the BIA, you know that they'll try to drill a subservient mentality into you; and in the towns, the discrimination is pretty bad."

La Nada again spent time working with her father, a former tribal chairman. They sent out letters to congressmen and senators describing conditions on the reservations, and tried to get the Bureau of Indian Affairs office to respond. As a result, her father was harassed by local law enforcement officials. La Nada drifted for a time and then asked the BIA for "relocation" off the reservation. Many of the Fort Hall Indians have taken this route and 80 percent of them return to the reservation, because, as La Nada says, "things in the slums where you wind up are even worse than on the reservation, and you don't have people to support you."

The BIA gave her a one-way ticket to San Francisco, one of eight major relocation centers in the country. When she first arrived, she sat in the local BIA office from 8 to 5 for a few days, waiting for them to help her find a job. They didn't, and she found a series of temporary clerk jobs by herself. As soon as she found work, the BIA cut off her $140 a month relocation payment. She wound up spending a lot of time in the "Indian bars" which are found in San Francisco and every other relocation town. She worked as a housekeeper in the private home for Indian girls where the BIA had first sent her, and as a barmaid in a beer parlor. She was "drunk most of the time," and she became pregnant. She was 17 years old.

"After I had the baby," she says, "my mother came out from the reservation and got him. She said they'd take care of him back home until I got on my feet. I really didn't know what to do. The only programs the BIA has are vocational training for menial jobs, and I didn't especially want to be a beautician. Actually, I wanted to try college again, but when I told this to a BIA counselor, he said they didn't have any money for that and told me I was being 'irrational and unrealistic.'

"All types of problems develop when you're on relocation. The Indian who has come to the city is like a man without a country. Whose jurisdiction are you under, the BIA's or the state's? You go to a county hospital when you're sick and they say, 'Aren't you taken care of by the Indian Affairs people?' It's very confusing. You hang around with other Indians, but they are as bad off as you are. Anyway, I started sinking lower and lower. I married this Sioux and lived with his family awhile. I got pregnant again. But things didn't work out in the marriage, and I left. After I had the baby, I ended up in the San Francisco General psychiatric ward for a few weeks. I was at the bottom, really at the bottom. Indian people get to this point all the time, especially when they're relocated into the big city and are living in the slums. At that point, you've got two choices: either kill yourself and get it all over with—a lot of Indians do this—or try to go all the way up, and this is almost impossible."

As she looks at it now, La Nada feels she was "lucky." She tried to get admitted to the local colleges, but was refused because of her school record. Finally, because the University of California "needed a token Indian in its Economic Opportunity Program for minority students," she was admitted in the fall of 1968. She did well in her classes and became increasingly active, helping to found the United Native Americans organization and working to get more Indian students admitted into the EOP program. "After my first year there," she says, "everything was going along all right. I liked school and everything, and I felt I was doing some good. But I felt myself getting swallowed up by something that was bigger than me. The thing was that I didn't want to stop being an Indian, and there were all these pressures, very hidden ones, that were trying to make me white." At the summer break she went back to the reservation and spent some time with her family. The next quarter she became involved in the Third World Liberation Front strike at Berkeley, fighting for a school of Ethnic Studies, including a Native American program. She was suspended by the University.

La Nada's experiences, far from being extreme cases, are like those of most young Indians. If she is unique at all, it is because she learned the value of fighting back.

8

FROM

The New Indians

by Stan Steiner

In 1953 the United States Congress formally adopted a policy of "termination" in its relations with the American Indian. This policy is stated in a crucial sentence of House Concurrent Resolution 108 (83rd Congress, 1st Session) which reads: "Resolved by the House of Representatives (The Senate concurring), that it is declared to be the sense of Congress that, at the earliest possible time, all the Indian tribes and the individual members thereof (located in four states, and certain specified tribes in addition) should be freed from federal supervision and control. . . ."

This resolution totally reversed the federal policy toward Indians as expressed in the Indian Reorganization Act of 1934. The Reorganization Act had been a milestone in Indian Affairs. It provided that no tribal lands should be parcelled out in individual allotments as had been the previous procedure. Annual authorizations of $2,000,000 for the purchase of tribal land was established. Credit funds for incorporated tribes were set up. Loans for vocational training and academic study were provided. Tribes were to be aided in the adoption of written forms of government. Indians were encouraged to obtain jobs in the Indian office. Conservation of Indian resources was pledged.

Although funds to enact many of these provisions were never fully appropriated, the policies established by the Act were very favorable to the Indian. The powers of the tribes as self-governing units were well established. The tribe became a significant economic organization for the Indians, collectively giving members the potential ability to hold large areas of land, to invest tribal monies, to establish industry, and to operate large-scale agricultural projects.

The termination policy severely crippled the social and economic growth of the American Indians. The tribe was destroyed as a powerful economic unit; land and capital was distributed to individuals, leaving them with little resources and power. Social disintegration of the tribe tended to follow termination.

Concurrent with the termination policy was the Relocation Program. Relocation, begun in 1950, was a program designed to take Indians off the reservation and place them in America's cities. It represented an attempt on the part of white administrators to quickly solve the government's "Indian problem" by forcing assimilation, by making the Indian disappear. The combined effects of termination and relocation were disastrous for the Indian.

In the following selection Stan Steiner examines the effects of these programs on the lives of Indians who went to the cities. The disorientation these transposed people face in America's cities is unimaginable to a white American. The adjustments which rural tribal people must make in attempting to cope with life in urban centers are overwhelming. In his essay Mr. Steiner shows both the successes and the failures of life in the cities for the "new Indians."

Stan Steiner's interest in the American Indian reaches back for more than twenty years. As a young man in 1946 he left New York City to explore the American West. He was, he states, "seeking after the source of my country and of myself." He found what he was seeking through the Indians he met and came to know.

The New Indians is the product of years of travel among Indians throughout the country. Published in 1968, the book is, according to the author, "an attempt to translate the thoughts of the Indian into the words of the white man."

* * *

Are the city Indians invisible?

The tribal Indians are unquestionably coming to town. Half of the Indians in the country may be city Indians, Vine Deloria, Jr., has estimated. There are a quarter of a million living in the metropolitan areas alone, thought Mel Thom [a young activist, tribal chairman of the Piute Walker River Reservation, and a founder and past president of The National Indian Youth Council]. And the San Francisco Indian Center publication *The American Indian,* has reported that the Indian adults living "off-reservation"—estimated at 198,000—outnumbered those "on-reservation"; for many job-seeking parents left their children at home with grandparents.

One decade ago, the *Harvard Law Review* estimated that "about 100,000 Indians [reside] in American cities and towns" ("American Indians: People Wthout a Future," by Ralph Nader, May 19, 1956). Even if the statistic was a reasonably inaccurate guess, the urban population of tribesmen has doubled within ten years.

But the city Indians have always been invisible statistics. The U.S. Census Bureau counts Indians only when they so identify themselves, or are identifiable. And the city Indians often "pass" as whites, when it is economically necessary, or socially desirable. Those who don't "pass" have been usually counted as "nonwhite"—a nearly invisible shade, it seems, when they happen to be Indians.

The statistics of the Bureau of Indian Affairs have been as equalitarianly invisible, for the Bureau's concern has traditionally been the reservation Indian, and the cajoling of him to leave the reservation. Once he goes, however, the Bureau no longer counts him.

So the city Indian has been an invisible man. He has not even become a statistic.

"Chicago does not realize they have a 'reservation of Indians' right in their own backyard," commented an official of the American Indian Center on the near North Side. "There are better than ten thousand Indians representing seventy tribes in Chicago." Half of these are wedged into a few-block area between the Puerto Rican ghetto and the luxury apartment houses on the Lake Shore Drive.

"We don't riot," said Nathan Bird, one of the Chicago Indian leaders, "so no one knows we're here."

Brooklyn, New York, Cleveland, Detroit, St. Louis, Minneapolis, Omaha, Denver, Phoenix, Los Angeles, San Francisco, and Seattle all have their own "native quarters" of Indians. Many of these have more than ten thousand tribal residents. And in the smaller cities of the Rocky Mountains, the Plains, and the Southwest, there are repetitious "Hill 57's." "The Cement Prairies" was what some of the city Indians nicknamed these homeless homes away from home.

In a tongue-in-the-throat article entitled "The Indian in Suburbia," *The American Indian* offered its own tourist guide to tribesmen coming to town:

When an Indian family first comes to Oakland, or San Francisco, they will find thousands of cement streets running in every direction.

On these streets will be tens of thousands of automobiles. These automobiles are filled with people who are trying to kill each other off with these steel monsters as fast as the white man killed off the Buffalo.

To find his way around in this cement prairie, the white man uses a map, and so must the Indian.

All of the houses have numbers and some of the streets are called by numbers. Some streets have other names, and in many cases streets are not called streets but avenues, places, boulevards and freeways. Freeways are the most dangerous and no one walks on them, and sometimes it is even hard to drive on them. . . .

And yet they come, in bemused bewilderment, and in growing migrations.

In the eyes of an Indian what does the city look like? He has seen villages and he has seen towns. Nowhere has he seen one million people, five million, living in houses like great tombstones, row upon row, and running about like little mechanical ants, to and fro, on streets full of cars like plagues of grasshoppers. He has lived most of his life without a side-walk, without a subway, without a superhighway, and often without a supermarket.

He has lived beside the still waters.

Living in the city is then not something he can adjust to with a street map, an orientation course, and a job. It is beyond his imagination, beyond his emotion.

Within a few miles of the metropolitan areas of Los Angeles and New York City more human beings live than in the more than one million square miles of all the states of the Western mountains and plains and deserts, where most of the tribal Indians come from.

So the tribesmen come into the metropolis with its glass and steel office buildings, where the twentieth century is on perpetual display like a living museum piece.

How exotic are the artifacts of the urban civilization! Its rituals of folk-rock chants, commercial ceremonials, and automobile worship were fascinating. The tribal Indians come with the curiosity of tourists. It is like visiting a circus in a foreign country.

Richard McKenzie, a young Sioux who lived in San Francisco for several years—successfully—and was a leader of the Indian Center in that city, cast a dubious eye on this citifying of the tribesmen. "The reservation Indian has not been prepared to make his way in the city of 1860s—much less the demanding fast-paced and cold-blooded city of 1960s," he said.

Life in the city whetted the Indian's curiosity, McKenzie said, but he faced a "hopeless situation." Most of the Indians he met were lost. "The simplest facts of life in the city were new to them: gearing your entire day by a clock, when to go to work, when to eat lunch. They don't even understand where you board a bus, how to pay, and how to open and close the doors.

"Because they have been sent from the reservation with the lack of training, information, and money," he said, they would be victims of "the hardships and loneliness of the disillusioned Indian in the city."

Why then, if the city Indian faces a "hopeless situation," do more and more rural Indians come to the cities?

"Lots of the younger kids want to leave the reservation and get a job," said Mary Lou Payne, a Cherokee girl who made the journey to the city herself. "It's not that they really want to get away from the reservation, but that they want to have an income. Everyone is *encouraged* to go away. To leave. To become a working American. To join the 'rat race,' really. What they call the 'mainstream.' "

The exodus has been not wholly voluntary. "It reflects a policy the Bureau of Indian Affairs has had and still has: to get the Indians off the reservation," Mary Lou Payne said.

"Relocation" is the term given to this trek. It was instituted by Commissioner of Indian Affairs Dillon Myer, who, as has been noted, was director of the Relocation Centers where Japanese-Americans were imprisoned during World War II. Thus, the term had a disquieting connotation to young Indians, many of whom had fought in that war. Nonetheless, tens of thousands of tribal Indians have been "relocated" since the early 1950s.

Hubert Humphrey has written optimistically about the "Relocation" Program: It is aimed at "encouraging Indians to move off the less promising reservations and into industrial centers where work opportunities are more plentiful. . . . A package program—vocational training and job placement, with all expenses paid for trainee and family—has lured 50,000 Indians into successful urban living."

The former Commissioner of Indian Affairs, Philleo Nash, who guided the program during the administration of the late President John F. Kennedy, was more cautious and less optimistic: "Relocation by itself solves nothing," Nash said. ". . . As long as relocation was merely a program to transport people from one pocket of poverty to another, little was accomplished. Not everyone likes city living—not everyone is suited to it. To combat poverty successfully will require programs that relate people to jobs wherever they choose to live."

Some of the relocated Indians were even more skeptical.

The Sioux, Richard McKenzie said that when a reservation Indian arrived in San Francisco he was referred by the Relocation Office to "the few boarding houses available to Indians under the Bureau program [that were] usually ill-run, often short on food, and in bad districts—especially for girls."

The jobs that the Bureau found for "the usually unskilled Indians" were often with "fly-by-night outfits who enjoy getting as much labor as possible from their workers while paying them as little as possible," McKenzie said. Since the Indians did not know union rules, many were working up to twelve hours a day without overtime pay. When "the pitifully small cash given to him to make the trip" ran out, the relocated Indian was often penniless and lost.

His own family, McKenzie said, had housed and fed "many Indians who were in dire need, but somehow did not qualify for aid from any [welfare] agency."

"Mr. Indian," said the irate Sioux, "your 'Green Pastures' in the city will be even worse than what you have now at home. Sending Indians [to the city] on a sink or swim basis is the way to guarantee most will sink."

"It was shameful," Mary Lou Payne said, "to force rural Indians into urban ghettos. It's no answer to poverty to dump these people into the cities. They are so unprepared for city life, paying bills every month, going to work every day, that they filter out to the very bottom of society.

"This shipping out of unprepared people is just shameful. It doesn't work out. They just go back to what they did before. Which is picking up odd jobs. But doing it in the cities."

Hubert Humphrey sounded an official note of concern: "Most of them [those Indians who go on their own] have never held jobs of any duration and are almost totally unequipped for industrial work. They seek to escape from poverty on the reservation without realizing that they may be making another and worse trap for themselves. Unless we take measures to help this group, we will find new ghettos being established in our cities and towns, new slum children growing up, a new breed of unemployed unemployables, taxing our welfare services."

Measures had to be taken immediately. . . .

Relocation had become a fancy word for "dumping the rural poor into the ghettoes," said Mel Thom. The idea of urbanizing and integrating the tribal Indian was forgotten, momentarily, and practical reality was recognized by changing the name of the Bureau of Indian Affairs, Branch of Relocation, to Branch of Employment Assistance.

The Vocational Education Act for Indians was intensified when Congress increased the appropriation from $12 to $15 million. Under this act, originally part of the Relocation Program, tribal Indians were job-trained and paid to leave their reservations. Yet, in the first ten years of its operation, but thirteen thousand of the tens of thousands of Indians who went to the cities benefited from its largess. "Usually Indians must leave the reservation to take advantage of it," *Eyapaha,* the Rosebud Sioux newspaper, complained.

Mary Lou Payne was less polite: "I have gripes about the on-the-job training programs. On the Cherokee Reservation back home we have two factories. One of them is a stitching plant, they make bed clothing; and the other is a bobby pin factory. They run the Indian kids through the training courses, the government picks up part of their salary while they're training, and then when they're through training, the company employs them for a month, or two months, and drops them, and hires another crew for training.

"How many jobs are there on the Cherokee Reservation where they can go and make stitched bed clothing? It's so impractical. They should be trained to become plumbers, carpenters, electricians, television repairmen."

Joe Maday, a young Chippewa boy on the Bad River Reservation in Wisconsin, had just come home from an on-the-job-training project, two thousand miles from his home.

He sat in his father's gas station, on a muddy river flat, near the wild-rice fields of his tribe on Lake Superior. He reminisced and he cursed the government for sending him to Seattle.

"Couldn't they send me to Milwaukee?" the boy said. He had gone wide-eyed and eager to see the country, on a $130-a-month government allowance, paying $90 a month for boarding-house rent. "Who could live on what was left? That rent for a dormitory-type room," he said. But it was exciting, anyway, being with Indians from a dozen tribes he had never heard of. "It was like a big powwow all the time. It didn't ever stop."

What did he learn? "Nothing!" he shrugged. "They wanted to teach me mechanics. But I didn't want to work as a mechanic way out there. So far away from home. And mechanics are a dime a dozen around here. So I come back. I'm going to learn electronics this time. If there's a job around here, I rather stay. But maybe I will go away. There's no work here. No one stays."

In spite of the newer urban-orientation course that had been started the tribal Indians still seemed disoriented by city life. So it was decided to urban-orientate them twice. Upon their arrival in the cities, the Bureau of Indian Affairs began to offer them a secondary education course in the rituals and customs of urban living.

Dr. Sophie D. Aberle and the late William A. Brophy, in *The Indian: America's Unfinished Business,* described one of these advanced courses:

"Orientation courses for Eskimos and reservation Indians unfamiliar with the manners and customs of life outside their villages have been started in Seattle, Washington. The three-week course is based on the assumption that the quickest way for students to adjust to modern life is to let them use up-to-date conveniences. . . .

"The training center is, therefore, located in a modern motel. Seven furnished apartments are rented for the trainees and their families. . . . All accommodations have carpeted floors, draperies, an all-electric kitchen, private bath and living rooms.

"It is too early to evaluate the results of the orientation or pre-vocational training courses," the authors wrote. "However, methods of teaching have been developed and are being studied by psychologists, psychiatrists, linguists, and other specialists, so that improvements are being constantly made."

When oriented the Indians were moved out of the all-electric kitchens and the wall-to-wall-carpeted motel suites to the nearest ghetto. The transition was jarring. "One Indian woman in Cleveland didn't know how to light a gas stove," Mary Lou Payne related, "and a welfare worker who visited her walked in and found this woman standing in the middle of her kitchen and throwing matches into the oven."

In the ghetto of Puerto Rican Harlem, the Barrio of Nueva York, lives a very different sort of city Indian. Her name is Princess Wa Wa Chaw—Mrs. Bonita Nuñez.

She was one of the earliest of the city Indians in New York, and she is now one of the oldest. In the cluttered memories of her rooms, high in a municipal housing project, are stacks of boxes full of history: souvenirs of the days when she danced with Isadora Duncan; her painting of Joe Gould, the Greenwich Village poet and eccentric; invititations to the White House; mementos of the vaudeville stage; books on the mysteries of the occult; and news stories of tours and arrests in the Indian-rights fight of fifty years ago.

"When I came here I was one of the first," the old woman said. "I 'came out' [off the reservation] so long ago. I lived on the Lower East Side for some time. The Jews from Europe had never seen an Indian before. There was quite a commotion. But we became good friends. Sometimes I don't know who has had it worse—the Jews or the Indians.

"The Negroes talk about discrimination. In those days there was worse discrimination in the cities against Indians. 'Savages' they called us then."

The old woman is very old, how old she would not say. She was born a Rincon Indian, in California, and was adopted by a white family at birth. "It was before the earthquake in San Francisco," was all she would say. She was on the stage at the age of ten. She lived all her life in the world of the white man. She knew no other life.

"Oh, I had friends everywhere. I could sing and act and dance and paint. I was not afraid," she recalled. "But you see I am still an Indian. Should the Indians be afraid of the city? No, the 'mainstream' should not frighten us. I am an existentialist," the old woman said.

Huddled under a shawl, in her modern apartment in the New York City housing project, she looked out on the defaced walls of the cold slums below her window and thought of one day long ago.

"One day I was walking down the street when a lady stopped me. She looked me in the eye. Then she hit me in the face. 'Go back where you came from! You foreigner!' she shouted. She was Italian, I think. But I was a brown Indian, you see." She sighed: "I am aware that [we] can become victims of the 'lonely people.' . . ."

Who in the city talks to strangers? The "lonely people" prefer to talk to their machinery; for didn't they say "the medium is the message?" Kathryn Polacca, a Navajo teacher who has been to many cities, said: "Your people have so many ways of communication: IBM machines, telephones, newspapers, telegraphs, radios, and television. In the Navajo ways the most important communication is still person to person. This is the way we solve many of our problems. This is the way we enjoy life." The Indian way of talking and living she said, was based on human values, not on mechanical or monetary values.

Unlike so many newcomers to the cities the tribal Indians "are not with it," Mel Thom said. "He doesn't think of making money. He just wants to make a living and live." That is why, though there are an estimated twenty thousand Indians in the environs of San Francisco, and perhaps thirty thousand in Los Angeles, Thom said he knew of only two or three Indian-owned establishments in either city. One was a bar.

"Money! Money! Money! That is all the white man thinks

of when it comes to the Indian," said a Pomo Indian of California. "The only thing they see is money. For me a heartbeat is enough. . . ."

It was not violence that these Indians feared. Guns and shooting do not frighten them. The urban man lives in terror of a hunting rifle on the ordered, policed, shattering quiet of the city street; the Indian does not. Hunting is a household commonplace to Indian youth. Rather it was the inhumanity of the mass killings that frightened the Indians. The cold-blooded way in which urban man would kill strangers to him for no emotional reason, with no feelings.

"Why do they kill like that?" an Oklahoma Cherokee, who regularly went home to hunt, asked. "I would not shoot deer that way."

Those Indians who chose to stay in the "cold-blooded city" had to protect themselves—politically, economically, and culturally. They were often abandoned by the federal bureaus, with little knowledge of the city agencies, left on their own, uncomfortable with urban life, separated from their tribes, and something had to be done for them, by themselves. The invisible city Indian had to become visible.

Where Indians have come, they have built Indian centers. The men and women from tribes throughout the country, with different cultures and different languages, would get together and establish a meeting place where they could meet relatives and tribesmen, reminisce about life back at home, discuss the frustrations of city life, and help and protect themselves. The Indian center might be a tiny, dreary storefront, or an elaborate and well-equipped community hall. But, whatever it looked like, it was run by and financed by tribal Indians, for tribal Indians.

Powwows in the city? A nostalgic attempt to transplant tribal life to the cement prairie? These Indian centers are not governmental or social-work-sponsored, not tribal nor intertribal. In coming to these community halls the Indians come as Indians, not representing their tribes. The city Indians have created something new and independent and yet Indian. They speak of the "Indian language"—"Let's talk

Indian," they say; though there is, of course, no such language —and seek to preserve their "Indian traditions," and they dance in powwows, doing "Indian dances," and they fight for their "Indian rights."

In doing these things they are not only building an Indian urban community, but are building an Indian consciousness that is no longer tribal, but is extratribal. It too is an embryo of Indian nationalism.

Chicago's Indian Center, one of the oldest and largest of these urban, extratribal groups, is typical in its goals of most. Its aim is to help tribesmen in becoming "a functioning part of the social fabric of the city," while "sustaining cultural values perhaps uniquely their own."

The Indians of Chicago are seeking, in other words, to become urban citizens outwardly, but to remain Indians inwardly. And these Indians wish to do this not by urbanizing the tribal life, nor by tribalizing the urban life, but by combining both. Fascinating are the combinations. Rock 'n' roll and tribal dances. Potlatch dinners and auto-mechanic classes.

In the San Francisco Indian Center within an ordinary week there was: Tuesday—Indian dancing; Wednesday—ladies' sewing club, Indian arts and crafts, girls' ping-pong and boys' pool tournaments; Thursday—council meeting on job, housing, and welfare problems; Friday—modern ballet class and a powwow (singers and dancers were "paid with gas money"); Saturday—Children's health clinic and rock 'n' roll dance (music by The Enchanters).

And on Sunday there was a movie entitled *The Exiles*.

These programs are run with a tribal communality: "Our Center is operated by Indians for all Indians in the Bay Area. All help is voluntary. Everyone just comes and does whatever they think has to be done for improvement. There is no one sponsoring this organization. Indians work here not for profit, but to contribute their time for a preservation of our disintegrating culture and heritage."

In a similar spirit of tribalism the American Indian Center in Chicago declared: "The Center is an achievement of their own [the Indians'], and not something provided for Indians by others. . . . The Center is not a sort of missionary outpost of the urban majority. It is a grass-roots effort."

Yearly the Chicago Indian Center provides services for thousands of tribesmen, but since its members have "never been wealthy people" it is in a perpetual state of near bankruptcy. The Welfare Council of Chicago, to which it is affiliated, suggested that the comfortably endowed and well-known Hull House take over the administration of the Indian Center. Its financial problems would be solved, and it would benefit from professional social work management.

The Chicago Indian Center voted down the beneficent offer, to the surprise of the city fathers. It was like voting not to accept a Congressional appropriation.

Nathan Bird, an Indian woodworker, who was on the board of directors of the Indian Center, tried to explain: "The Hull House is a fine place. We have nothing against it. We were afraid that we would lose our identity if they took us over. It always happens. It would no longer be an Indian Center. The whites would take us over and tell us what to do. It was a bribe. We could use the money. We won't sell our Indian rights for money.

"That's what happens on the reservations," Mr. Bird said. "The government is always taking things over to 'help us.' We don't want that kind of 'help.' We didn't come all the way to Chicago for some more of that."

City Indians, because they are on their own—neither protected nor restricted by the Bureau of Indian Affairs—tend to be more independent and more outspoken. In Minneapolis the city Indians twice in two years picketed the Bureau's area office. Picketing, in itself, had been unknown to tribal movements; tribesmen would sooner take up a rifle in defense of their treaty rights than take up a picket sign. It was "un-Indian," the elders said.

But the Urban American Indian Protest Committee of the Twin Cities had no such fears. It was organized by two younger Indians, Mary Thunder and George Mitchell. On its first picket line it mustered thirty-five city Indians, who carried signs demanding that the government begin programs to help them. It had none, they said, and they demanded assistance in getting housing, jobs, and education; referral services for medical and legal care; and practical urban orientation programs. . . .

The invisibility of the city Indian belongs to the past. He is becoming visible. He may have been lost in the city; but the longer he has stayed the more he has begun to feel it is the city that is lost—not he. When the city Indian began to build urban tribal communities he discovered the Indian way of life filled the lonely void of "the cement prairies." And he began to wonder if "the lonely crowd" might learn neighborliness from him.

"The very values the Indian represents may contribute to the improvement of our frantic cities," said Richard McKenzie. He thought the values of tribal humanism might "make the cities more human." And one young Pueblo Indian in the Chicago Indian Center said: "Instead of giving Indians these urban-orientation courses, maybe they ought to give Chicagoans human-orientation courses."

Has the "alienation" of the city Indian been too convenient and self-comforting a concept? It has been used by non-Indians to define the feelings of the Indian, but it has described the effect and not the cause. It has placed the onus on the Indian for his failure to conform to urban life and for his return home to the reservation. But, at a time when the disappearance of communities and the demise of neighborhoods are troubling city planners, the communal feeling of the city Indian has something to be said for it.

If the "alienation" of urban life becomes too overwhelming, the city Indian returns to his tribal community, and home to the reservation many had gone.

"The return to the reservations," former Commissioner of Indian Affairs Philleo Nash, estimated, "was about as frequent as the permanent relocation." Mary Lou Payne thought it even greater: "On this relocation the return home is fantastic. I bet it is 60 percent and up who return to the reservations." Richard McKenzie said it was his experience that 90 percent return home as soon as there were jobs on the reservations.

A young girl of the Laguna Pueblo, Pat Pacheco, who returned to her pueblo from college, where she had studied psychology, said: "It's almost impossible to adjust to the outside world, and many of our people are coming back from Cleveland, Chicago, and Los Angeles, because they can work here now."

Not only are the relocated Indians beginning to go home, the *Wall Street Journal* observed, but "there's evidence Indians aren't moving off reservations as readily as a short while ago."

Into the Indian Center of San Francisco, up the shabby stairs, one day walked an unknown tribesman. He was welcomed, as every Indian was, a tall man, with a tight face and puzzled eyes. The man was a newcomer; perhaps he had just arrived from the reservation, and was ill at ease.

The stranger was something more, however. He was a relocation officer of the government who had been sent from the reservation to see how the tribal Indians were being urbanized.

"He was told we took a rather dim view of the program," a San Francisco Indian recalled. "I pinned him down about the lack of adequate orientation on the reservation. And he said they did indeed tell people about buses, housing, and so forth. I told him that John Glenn could tell me in six orientation lessons how to fly a space ship and I wouldn't know a thing about it if I got in one."

That broke up the official meeting. "Last three hours of our visit were spent talking about hunting, fishing, and wide-open spaces on the reservation. The cheaper cost of living and better life in general back home," the relocated Indian said. "Naturally, many of the things the relocation officer said, and many of the things he saw, will never be included in his written report to Washington, D.C., or for that matter in his verbal report to his superintendent on the reservation.

"One wonders, after seeing relocation at the other end, if he will not be more reluctant about sending Indian people out. Will the relocation officer relocate himself?" The city Indian laughed.

The most unusual tale of relocation-in-reverse, however, occurred in Los Angeles. In that multiplicity of the Angels lived a group of Cherokees. Some of the families were well established and some were well to do. They were all Los Angeles boosters; for they had done well enough and lived quite happily.

Yet the hills of eastern Oklahoma of the Cherokee Nation haunted them. "Twelve years ago a group of Indians, many of us children, or grandchildren, of Oklahomans, decided to 'put down a fire' in California," said Dr. John Harris Jeffries, a lawyer and chiropractic doctor who was a leader of these Los Angeles Cherokees. He explained that to "put down a fire" in the Cherokee tradition, meant just that. A ceremonial ground was prepared and a fireplace dug in the earth. There the fire was lighted for religious rituals. There a stomping ground for religious dances was established around the fire.

In the city of Los Angeles, the Western Keetoowah Society was founded. The Keetoowah Society is the nativist religious group of the Cherokees. Its traditional worship, with masks and robes and rites, was not only sacred, but in the urban frenzy was an island of the Indian spirit. Though the city Cherokees were separated by miles of freeways, they held regular religious ceremonies and prayers. In the kinship families they kept their matriarchal clans intact. The old customs of the tribe were practiced, and the children given Cherokee names in the traditional way.

One of the Western Keetoowah Society of Los Angeles members was a lawyer. One was an insurance salesman. One was the owner of an electrical firm. One was a professional golfer. One was a professional artist. One was a surveyor. One was a doctor. One was a computer analyst. And yet—business suits off, ties loosened, brief cases left in the foyers of the suburban houses—they were traditionalist Indians.

"Suddenly we began to think about coming home," Dr. Jeffries said. "I don't know with whom the idea originated.

We knew we wanted to get out of the rat race in Los Angeles. There just wasn't any discussion about where we should go. It was Tahlequah."

And so to Tahlequah, Oklahoma, the old capital of the Cherokee Nation, the families began to come. In the beginning just seven families moved. Then four more came. Soon forty of the Cherokees had come. Dr. Jeffries expected that in all one hundred and fifty would come home.

"It was home instantly," he said. "No one has mentioned moving back." Somehow it was as though they had never left.

The coals of the sacred fires that they had "put down" in Los Angeles were unearthed. In their cars the coals were carefully carried halfway across the continent, once more to be buried, but this time in the earth of their Cherokee homeland. Once more, the fires would flame.